HEARST MARINE BOOKS
SEA KAYAKING
BASICS

HEARST MARINE BOOKS
SEA KAYAKING
BASICS

David Harrison

Illustrations by Ron Carboni

HEARST MARINE BOOKS

New York

Library of Congress Cataloging-in-Publication Data

Harrison, David, 1938–
    Hearst Marine Books sea kayaking basics / David Harrison.
        p.   cm.
    Includes index.
    ISBN 0-688-12243-4
    1. Sea kayaking.   I. Title.   II. Title: Sea kayaking basics.
GV788.5.H37   1993
796.1'224—dc20   93-22637
                                                         CIP

Printed in the United States of America

        3   4   5   6   7   8   9   10

EDITED BY MICHAEL MOULAND

BOOK DESIGN BY GIORGETTA BELL McREE

ACKNOWLEDGMENTS

Until recently, the books and manuals on the sport of kayak touring, or sea kayaking, as it is so glamorously called, have mostly been the product of the Brits and their disciples. I have read many of these works and am indebted to them for their pioneering efforts. These writers were adventurers first, instructors second, and writers by accident. The strength of the existing literature on sea kayaking lies in the résumés of the authors, most of whom have accomplished some notable sea voyages.

My own paddling résumé is longer on canoe tripping than on sea kayaking, but as the editor in chief of *Canoe* magazine, a periodical that has been covering sea kayaking for most of the magazine's twenty-year history, I have the good fortune to know many of the "credentialed" members of the sea kayaking fraternity. As befits pioneers—although indigenous peoples do have a few thousand years on them—they are an obstinately opinionated bunch. I have sat in on many a symposium and heard one expert express views on some facet or another that completely contradict those of the expert who just proceeded him or her. Sometimes their expertise borders on the metaphysical.

In this volume, I have sifted through the collective knowledge, experience, technique, instruction, and even the metaphysical offerings of the experts, added the sum of my own experience, and attempted to present kayaking as a balance somewhere between the easily attainable and the adventurous.

I have received guidance and advice from many people, but my special thanks go to Lee Moyer, proprietor of Pacific Water Sports, in Seattle, much of whose thinking I have borrowed heavily from. He also devoted many hours trying to root out the awkward, the misinformed, and the just plain erroneous in my original manuscript. If I overruled him in a few cases because of a difference of opinion, he gets no footnote; in other words, the final product is my responsibility.

Both Lee Moyer and Mike Neckar, proprietor of Necky Kayaks in Abbotsford, British Columbia, have tutored me on the subject of kayak design, and I trust they will pardon my overearnest efforts at simplification.

Many of the technique photos, including those that were converted into illustrations, are of Brent and Boo Turner, both of whom have extensive competitive experience. They enjoy sea kayaking, but it is their superlative technique, honed through race training, that sets a high standard for kayakers who wish to advance beyond elbow paddling.

The instructional format of this book is a synthesis of whitewater and sea kayaking techniques and drills gleaned from many sources: the instructors of Otter Bar Kayak School (Forks of Salmon, Calif.), Nantahala Outdoor Center (Bryson City, N.C.), Northwest Outdoor Center (Seattle) and Pacific Water Sports (Seattle). I have picked and chosen freely from them, so that the synthesis is wholly my own (in case any or all of them wish to distance themselves from my presentation).

CONTENTS

INTRODUCTION

The kayak, like its close relative the canoe, is a simple, primitive vehicle. Originally fashioned from natural materials—hides, skins, wood, bark, sinew, bone, and gut—the modern craft embody new technologies but no new ideas. The primitive vehicles were intended to be silent and stealthy (for hunting), portable, and able to be constructed from locally available materials. If the skin and bone and sinew, and bark and logs, were available in sufficient quantity and quality today, we might still be paddling skin boats and wooden canoes. Modern manufacturers attempt to replicate many of the good qualities of the original materials in their designs today: light weight, flexibility, stress resistance, and quiet. The only new idea may be large-scale production.

Of course, those original canoes and kayaks were meant for work: hauling, fishing, and hunting. They were the trucks and trains of antiquity. They were also the vehicles of war in certain realms. Martin Frobisher, one of the earliest Europeans to touch North America, was set upon by spear-wielding natives in the bay that now bears his name on the southern tip of Baffin Island. The Aleuts launched thousand-kayak navies, which the Russians called *bidarkas.* The inland and coastal Indians mastered guerrilla operations using canoes.

Some say that kayak racing originated the day the second kayak was built. Perhaps, but the idea of canoes and kayaks as vehicles for recreation and fun, not transportation, is a modern one. There are a few outposts where kayaks or canoes are still used for work. They are used as vehicles for hunting and fishing, but generally not for subsistence—just sport.

Perhaps as a reaction to our crowded, noisy, mechanized times, primitive craft like the canoe and kayak are appearing on waters everywhere, even more numerous than the Aleut bidarka navies. These boats have a new role to play. They make a shrinking world grow larger. They are quiet, self-contained, unmotorized, and able to access the intimate byways and hideaways that are inaccessible to other modes of travel. Ed Gillet, a former yachtsman turned kayaker who made history and brief notoriety when he paddled a kayak from Monterey, California, to the Hawaiian Islands, said it well: "Instead of spending $100,000 on a boat, a slip, and maintenance to visit a few new harbors, I can take my relatively inexpensive kayak anywhere I can drive, fly, sail, or paddle, and explore places most yachtspeople see only through their binoculars."

Modern materials, increasing demand by recreationalists looking for an ecologically compatible activity, and cost-effective production methods have made available a huge array of boats in every conceivable size, shape, and usage category. Color and, yes, even fashion, can be part of your quest as well. What the mountain bike did for the backroads the kayak does for the waterways (which in some places are the *only* ways). If the sheer motion pleasure—as in biking or cross-country skiing—doesn't thrill you, the exercise component will. Paddling can be a low-impact aerobic activity, if you wish to make it so. It is also a "backpack on the water," although no backpacker could ever carry the amenities that can be fitted into a touring kayak.

Originally popularized as a single-handed—and somewhat hairy-chested—activity for antisocial types, the kayak lends itself to family and group recreation. A tremendous variety of hulls and boat sizes can equalize the size and strength differences within a group. Big, stable, two-person kayaks bring partnership to the sport and can as well be used to team a stronger with a weaker paddler.

From your first paddle stroke and the gentle, free glide of a kayak hull over shimmering waters, you'll experience the exhilaration and sense the possibilities. The sensation springs from a craft that is so simple, so elemental, and from the places where waters run and hide, so infinite, that you will quite literally open up a whole new world to your physical and spiritual self.

HEARST MARINE BOOKS
SEA KAYAKING
BASICS

THE KAYAK AND ITS WATER

The kayak is an incredible invention. It can perform in ways no other water craft can match. In fairness, one should consider the capabilities of other small craft, since the kayak is not the only craft that meets the criteria of stealth, portability, and the ability to operate in waters from 4 inches to 25,000 feet deep. Canoes, dories, rafts, and various other rowing craft have all performed similar roles and adventured into all the environments suitable to kayaks. Some years back, two young women rowed a dory from Seattle to Skagway, Alaska, traveling up the so-called inside passage. That's also a trip that's been made by many kayakers. The women were members of the Dartmouth College women's crew, and they chose a custom-built craft that used their skills to best advantage. It obviously got the job done.

Many coastal voyages have been made in canoes, and for centuries canoes have traveled the huge lakes—call them inland seas—of Canada. (We can report that Lake Winnipeg, for example, is a more dangerous piece of water than Puget Sound.) In skilled hands, well-designed canoes can do much of what kayaks can do. Sitting high on a canoe seat affords good visibility (compared to the kayaker's fishlike vantage point); there's lots of room to move around and even stand up; and canoes are easier to load, unload, and carry on a portage. Besides all that, more people learned to canoe in the Boy Scouts or at summer camp than ever sat in a kayak. For trips on chains of lakes and rivers, where multiple portages and camps were in prospect, where capacity for large packs or bulky gear (like an ice cooler) or provision for a dog or a child is a factor, I'd likely choose a canoe.

So why choose a kayak? Some people think they look cool: long, sleek, so intimate with the water. Here, in fact, is why the kayak is the ultimate marriage of form and function. Because of the low profile, and because the paddler's center of gravity is lower, a narrow kayak will be as stable as a wide canoe, but be considerably faster—assuming that engines of equal power and comparable technical skills are pushing the paddle. Kayaking skills are, in fact, more easily learned, meaning that a nonpaddler will more quickly be able to make a kayak go forward in a straight line than a canoe. A double-bladed paddle, often a rudder, and a hull that tends to be more V-shaped (causing it to go more readily in a straight line) put even the novice quickly in control, as compared to the complexities of directing a canoe with pry strokes, C-strokes, J-strokes, or whatever.

Perhaps that should read "apparent control," since making forward progress in a straight line is only one element of control, albeit an extremely important one, as we will see as we progress through this manual. Dealing with wind and waves, launching and landing, avoiding obstacles—this calls for a number of other control skills. But, as it turns out, most of those skills are more easily mastered in the kayak, owing to its low center of gravity and double-bladed clout.

It's the wind and the waves that present the greatest challenges in any paddler's environment; a complete novice can usually make his boat go where he wants it to go on a quiet and protected body of water. The low profile of the craft and symmetry of the two-bladed paddle give the kayak a tremendous advantage over other types of paddle- and oar-powered craft when the elements begin to rumble. You are in an ideal position to compensate and react to turbulent conditions about you. People who spend time in large sailboats and powerboats are usually amazed at a kayak's ability to be on the water in conditions that would keep them at their anchorage. The fact is, a kayak can go where most other boats cannot.

Virtually any sea or touring kayak is capable of negotiating moderate whitewater rivers, big, slow-moving rivers, tidal estuaries, coastal bays, shorelines, inlets, lakes, inland seas (like the Great Lakes), and the open ocean. About 4 inches of water is all it takes; everything beyond that is only a matter of kayaker skill and experience.

Actually, it's a bit more complicated than that, as we will see in the following chapter. Some boats do some things better than others, and you, the paddler, have to do some serious self-assessment and master some basic skills.

FINDING YOUR KAYAK

There are two kinds of people: those who run up the "up" escalator and those who always stop to smell the flowers. And if these people are good at self-assessment, they will choose very different kayak designs. Most "experts" who write about boat design tend toward gross simplification, and so will I!

Long, skinny kayaks go fast and are tippy; short, fat boats are slow, but stable. Well, that's not a bad place to start. If, in fact, you are a flower smeller, bird watcher, fisherman, or are simply a less athletic or less aggressive person, you'll be a lot happier in a wide, stable boat that serves your transportation needs, not your cardiovascular system or libido.

But if you're the kind of person who can't stay at the end of a bicycle pace line for a full turn, or if you put a high premium on speed and performance—no matter what the sport—spring for the skinniest kayak that you can fit yourself and your gear into. For boats less than 23 inches wide, expect to put in ten hours of on-the-water paddling time for every inch of width *less* than that before you feel comfortable and at ease. This non-scientific proposal contains another piece of sage advice: if you expect to be only an occasional paddler—perhaps two weekends a year plus one seven-day trip—you'll be better off in a wider, higher-volume boat, no matter what your personality type or level of athleticism. Anxiety consumes energy, and that "tippy" feeling may leave you with less power for your paddle stroke if you failed to invest the necessary on-the-water time to master your high-performance kayak.

There's a school of kayak gurus who say skinny boats unencumbered by a rudder are best because they require the paddler to develop the skills that will keep him out of trouble. Other ex-

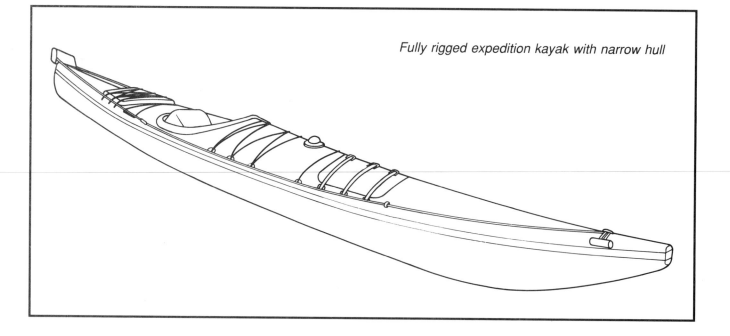

Fully rigged expedition kayak with narrow hull

perts argue that wide hulls, big cockpits, and boats with rudders provide insurance, because most of us are not athletes, just average human beings. Still others say that, regardless of boat type, the emphasis should be on seamanship and wise trip planning; paddling skills and fancy equipment are less important than understanding tidal currents or recognizing the approach of a storm.

Even if you ultimately choose a boat because it's the boat that all your friends paddle, there are a wide range of attributes worth knowing about. You needn't immerse yourself in the physics of boat hulls, but here are some observations on why kayaks do what they do.

HULL SHAPE

When boats were made from skin and sticks, designs were limited by materials. In the age of plastic and fiberglass, they are infinite. One designer's idea of perfection—a boat that surfs well, for example—may be contrary to the expectations of the expedition paddler who wants hull speed and load-carrying capacity. And the boat that races across the water empty, may plow into waves because it is submerged below its optimum waterline when fully loaded. The flat-bottomed hull that felt so stable on the dealer's test-paddle pond—this is referred to as "initial stability"—becomes awkward and slothful when the waves begin to toss.

Despite my earlier claim about the relative stability of a 23-inch-wide boat, there are 24-inch-wide kayaks that most people would have trouble keeping right side up, and there are 22-inch kayaks that most people would feel quite stable in. That's because *width* is simply one measurement, usually taken at the widest point of the boat. And that's why hull shape is important.

Round bottoms and deeply V'd bottoms are associated with performance kayaks. Yet a number of excellent touring kayaks are V-shaped at bow and stern; they do, however, widen considerably at the midsection, where the hull incorporates a rounded or shallow-arched shape. Such a hull might feel initially less stable than a flat-bottomed kayak, but when the boat is leaned over, the paddler has the sense of buoyancy and stability. Such boats are said to have good "final stability."

The underwater, longitudinal shape of the kayak will also affect performance and the paddler's sense of stability. Hulls are either symmetrical, Swede-form (widest point aft of the kayak's midpoint) or fish-form (widest ahead of the midpoint). It is often difficult to judge the hull shape by looking at the boat from the side or overhead, since the deck may incorporate a shape that has more to do with accommodating an efficient paddle stroke, or in the case of race boats, with meeting certain dimensional restrictions. Turn the boat over to determine the actual hull shape.

If, in fact, it matters. Here is another instance of experts disagreeing. There are as many proponents of fish-form hulls as there are the believ-

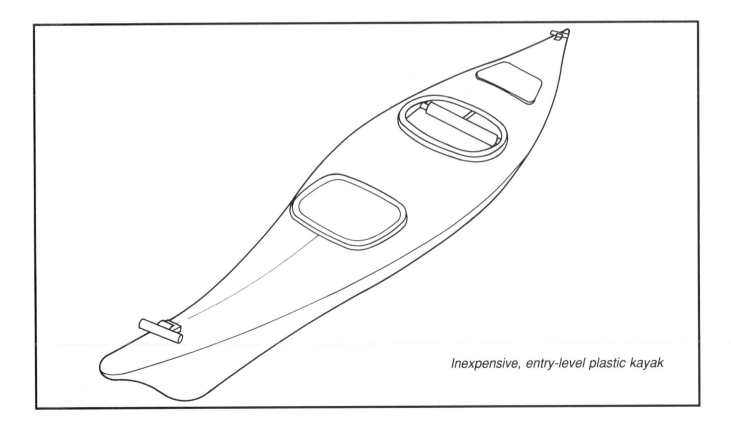

Inexpensive, entry-level plastic kayak

ers in Swede-form hulls, with each advocate capable of making a sure case for the superior efficiency (do they mean speed?) of their chosen design. The Swede-form hull would appear to cut through the water with it's rapier bow offering the least resistance. But the fish-form believer will say that a hole must first be punched in the water to pull the rest of the boat through. The fact is that no matter how rarified the science of hull physics has become, there are just too many variables when translating these into an actual kayak hull. Regardless of the hypothetical performance characteristics of that hull in the hands of paddler *x* and under wave and wind conditions *y,* the real paddler and conditions may be quite different. This may explain why most avid kayakers end up owning many boats, either trading one for another over time, or maintaining a stable full of them.

Accept the fact that hull design is more art than science, and we will press on. One of the theoretically important hull variables is length. Length may be used to predict *potential* hull speed, and the calculus says longer is faster because a long boat makes less of a bow wave (which the paddler and his boat must climb). This is true up to a point. Beyond, say, 20 feet, the drag, or friction, created by a long hull has more negative effect on speed than does a minimal bow wave. Also, from a practical standpoint, most recreational paddlers seldom exceed 3 knots at a normal paddling pace, and at such slow speeds friction is more important than wave making. The conclusion: a shorter boat (under 17 feet) may be a more efficient, more maneuverable craft for most people. It is certainly more portable.

Stiff, straight-tracking hulls, which are more V-shaped, contribute to speed and paddling efficiency, too, but there is usually a trade-off between straight tracking, on the one hand, and maneuverability, or ease of turning, on the other. An important design element in whitewater kayaks, where quick turning is critical, is "rocker." That's the amount of rise in the keel line toward the ends of the boat. Sea kayaks are about 50 percent longer than whitewater kayaks and generally have less than 4 inches of rocker—measured from floor to keel at the bow and stern—since straight-ahead paddling is the norm, and rudders or a slight boat lean provide enough turning impetus for the touring environment. If you want a hybrid boat, which might see time on mild white water, some additional rocker and/or a shorter kayak would be a good idea.

THE DECK AND BOW SECTION

Above the waterline, that theoretical "line" along the side of your kayak that just touches the water are the bilges or gunwale line. Above that is the deck, whose simplest purpose is to cover the boat and provide depth which, in combination with the hull, gives the boat its volume and carrying capacity. Some decks are peaked near the cockpit and tapered toward each end. The peaked deck is designed to shed water and give the paddler a dry ride. Extreme examples of the so-called West Greenland–style kayak, taper toward the bow (less so toward the stern), then jut out like prows. Such designs are supposed to cut through waves and won't pearl (bury their noses) in the kelp. Since the upswept bow and stern are inherently unstable when the boat is upside down, they must, therefore, roll more easily. That's what fans of the West Greenland style say.

Those who design more simply tapered bows say "Nonsense"; the upswept bows are, at worst, wind catchers, and at best, an affectation whereby fiberglass mimics a style forced on the Eskimos by the nature of their building materials.

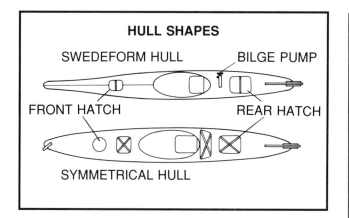

HULL SHAPES

SWEDEFORM HULL   BILGE PUMP

FRONT HATCH   REAR HATCH

SYMMETRICAL HULL

You can avoid taking sides by choosing a boat with only a modest upturn at the bow. A slicing bow makes sense, but it should widen quickly so as to ride up out of the wave troughs; and the deck (including the placement and shape of the front hatch) should be designed to shed waves to the side rather than let them wash up the deck to hit you between the eyes. Unless, of course, you are one of those sporty types who actually prefers mixing it up with the elements, just as some people prefer the hard, tight ride of a foreign sports car instead of the mushy ride of a big American sedan.

TOPLESS KAYAKS

Now that you know all about decks, you can think about so-called topless kayaks as well. There are a whole fleet of sit-upon kayaks, ranging from wide, stable, plastic boats to pencil-thin surf skis. The topless kayaks have a divot for your buttocks and heel wells. Many are designed to be "self-bailing" with one-way valves, or "scuppers," that drain water from the cockpit as you paddle. The long surf skis have foot-pedal-operated rudders.

Topless kayaks can do anything and go anywhere that decked kayaks can go. The wider plastic boats are often used as dive platforms or for ocean surfing. Surf skis range from wide rescue craft to the pure racing hulls that are raced the 30 miles across the huge swells of the Kalohi Channel, which separates the Hawaiian islands of Molokai and Lanai. Sit-on kayaks are obviously more appealing in warm climates, but if you have an aversion to crawling into cockpits and don't want to worry about "Eskimo rolling," topless kayaks may be for you. If you do happen to *huli* (Hawaiian for "turn over"), you simply clamber back on. Your topless kayak is just a big flotation chamber.

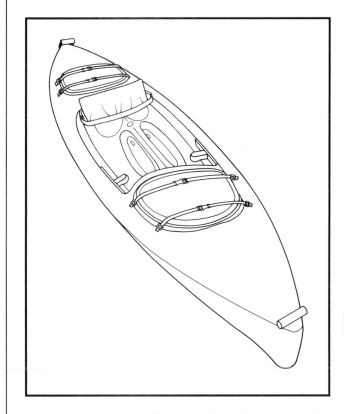

Topless or "sit-on-top" kayak with hatches, adjustable foot pegs, some models have thigh straps for control.

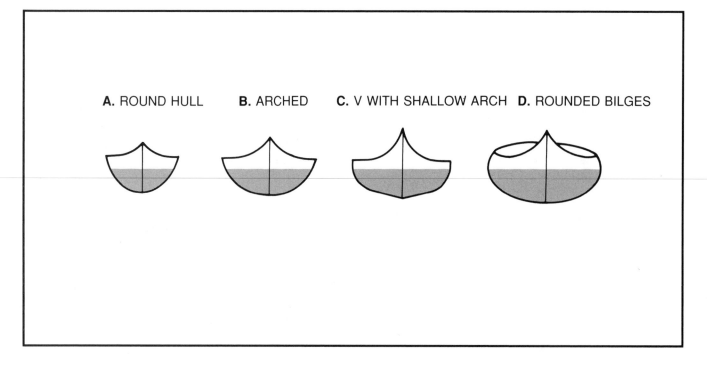

A. ROUND HULL   **B.** ARCHED   **C.** V WITH SHALLOW ARCH   **D.** ROUNDED BILGES

SINGLE OR DOUBLE

The sport of kayaking has been dominated by single-handed images. Many of us are attracted to the sport because of the idea that we can single-handedly carry and paddle, come and go, almost as we please. Escalator runners and flower sniffers can coexist on the same outing if the runners will remember to wait up or circle back now and then. While one group may choose to stay in camp, have another cup of coffee, or hang out on the beach, another will grab their kayaks and circumnavigate the island before lunch. In the evening the one angler in the group will paddle out to the channel and drop his line.

No doubt about it: The single kayak can provide personal satisfaction and freedom; but couples, or families, should consider a double kayak. They tend to be extraordinarily stable and quite fast. Most are 20 or more feet long, and when pushed by four paddle blades they usually leave the singles in their wake. But the greatest advantage of a double is the capability of teaming a strong and a weak paddler so that no one gets left behind.

If kayak camping is one of your objectives, consider the carrying capacity of doubles versus singles. Double kayaks invariably get to carry the two-burner stove and the five-gallon water jugs because the overall dimensions of a double kayak—especially those with center storage—result in larger cargo areas. There are a number of

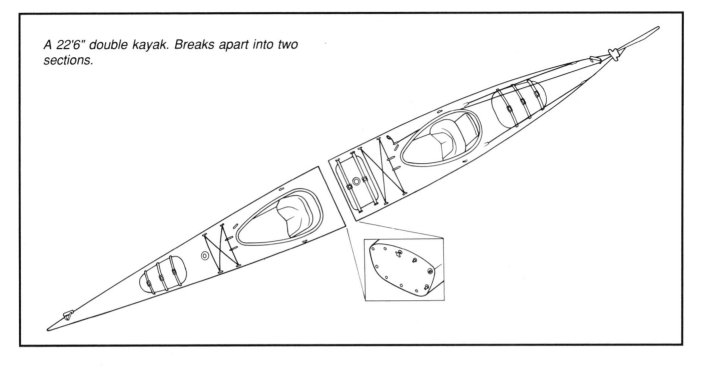

A 22'6" double kayak. Breaks apart into two sections.

giant doubles on the market that can accommodate two weeks' gear, and a small child can be positioned in the center hatch. Nevertheless, one double kayak will usually have less total carrying capacity than two singles because you're missing the equivalent of one stern section (or bow section, if you prefer).

KAYAKS FOR WOMEN

If this subhead appears to be an afterthought, it is not intended to be. In fact, the available data suggests that there are more women participating in sea kayaking than men. That's for good rea-

son. Apart from getting the boat on and off a car roof—which may influence your choice of boat—kayaking is not a strength sport but a skill sport. A 90-pound woman with a good strength-to-weight ratio can match any male paddler on the water. And if you are not ninety pounds, there's other good news. Women tend to have a greater proportion of their weight below the waist than do men, which translates into an even lower CG (center of gravity) for women. Most instructors will affirm the quicker speed with which women master the skills. Sometimes that's just because they listen more carefully, but it is also because, as they tend to be more flexible and have a better kinesthetic sense, they are quick to recognize that mastering the strokes is a matter of finesse, not brute strength.

A woman's lower CG may be reason enough for a woman to consider smaller volume, narrower kayaks and enjoy a lighter boat as a consequence. The narrower boats permit an easier reach with the paddle and may provide just enough hull-speed advantage to cancel out the strength advantage of a male paddling companion. Of course, a woman may choose a wide, stable kayak for the same reason as a man: she wants a platform for shooting pictures or bird watching. The bottom line is that females will have to go through the same selection process as males, and not every woman is going to want a wide, flat-bottomed barge that can only be sunk by a direct hit from an ocean freighter.

PARTS, PIECES, AND APPENDAGES

No matter how much tech-speak you are subjected to by dealers, kayak designers, kelp heads (the sea kayak equivalent of "gear heads" in bicycling), and expert writers, never forget that the Eskimos and Aleuts mastered their challenging environments quite nicely without an ounce of plastic or stainless steel. You can buy a simple kayak—no bulkheads, no rudder, no hatches, no deck lines—stuff your gear into each end, and paddle up the coast to Alaska tomorrow. Your seamanship and paddling skills will be the key to your success, not the prismatic coefficient of the hull, or your kayak's rudder retraction system (if it has one).

That said, let's look at a host of features and accessories that can make a difference in your comfort, your efficiency, and even your safety. Some will also affect your pocketbook.

Cockpit and Spray Skirt

Unless you've chosen a topless kayak, your kayak will have a cockpit (or two), and its perimeter will form a lip around which a spray skirt will snap by means of an elastic cord sewn into the hem of the spray skirt. The size of the cockpit is an important consideration. The largest cockpits make it easy to load gear through the cockpit; you can enter and exit easily, and you may just enjoy a less claustrophobic feeling. Very small cockpits require that you squirm in and out, and you can't draw your knees up until you are out of the boat. However, small kayaks are favored by aggressive paddlers who want their kayak to be fitted to them more like a ski boot. Like whitewater paddlers, they expect to be dealing with rough conditions, and an Eskimo roll is part of their repertoire.

In the next chapter I'll describe the spray skirts that snap around your cockpit, but for now we'll just sit in the open cockpit. Some seats will match your anatomy and some won't, and you won't know until you sit in the seat for a while, preferably paddling in it for a half hour or more. Not to worry; if you ultimately find that your perfect kayak has an imperfect seat, minicell foam can be used to reshape the offending contour.

Back support is important; make sure your kayak has an adjustable backrest or firm back band. You will also appreciate having some storage space and easy access behind your seat and in front of your foot pegs for packing the gear you want to get at without opening the hatches. More on that when we discuss bulkheads and hatches.

Foot Pegs and Thigh Braces

If your kayak has no rudder, you will still need foot pegs, which adjust to your leg length and give you something solid to push against; foot pegs are the final component of your transmission system, which includes arms, torso, buttocks, and legs. Good foot brace systems permit you to make the adjustment while seated in the cockpit. The foot pegs become the rudder controls in kayaks with rudders. Thigh braces are usually integral with the inside of the cockpit, especially smaller ones, and they permit you to go into a "brace lock" position for solid boat leans and Eskimo rolls. For a good transmission system, you want to have the foot pegs shortened to force your knees and thighs up and into the thigh braces, and if you are planning for aggressive paddling, you should also consider adding "hip clips": foam pads on each side of the seat, for an even more secure hold. Most paddlers will just want some well-positioned padding on the underside of the deck or cockpit.

Rudders and Skegs

In the technique chapters, we'll go over all the ways to turn and control the direction of your kayak—without using a rudder, which should tell you that they are not an essential. A few kayak makers insist that their designs shouldn't be encumbered with a rudder, claiming that they track well without them, that they are just one more piece of equipment subject to breakdown and paddlers should learn skills that obviate their need.

In truth, the primary goal of a rudder is not to turn the kayak, but to keep it in a straight line. For those of us who favor the installation of a rudder on a kayak, it adds just one more element of control and becomes almost an automatic pilot, keeping you on course as you settle into a rhythmic, half-conscious paddling state. On calm waters, leave the rudder up, and put it down when a combination of wind and waves demands too many correcting strokes, boat leans, or other adjustments. That's when you want to put your principal energy into forward strokes, not course correction.

Regardless of your final decision—rudder or no rudder—on your single kayak, a double kayak is almost unmanageable without a rudder. Major weight differences between the bow and stern paddler, the extra length and likelihood of big loads, as well as the problems of coordinating the partners in boat leans and paddle strokes, all dictate a good rudder system for a double. The usual practice is to put the controls in the rear of the double, but there is no reason that you couldn't arrange for rudder controls to be moved into the forward cockpit.

Some rudders can be raised from the water and then lowered to a flush position on the rear deck by means of two lines. Very neat, but you need to remember which of the two lines is "up" versus "down," and be sure the rudder is on center line for retraction from the water: then, be ready for the thud when the rudder hits your deck. The rudder is less prone to damage in its retracted position, and the foot braces are locked in position. Upright rudders are not as elegant, but they are mechanically simpler—one tug on one line and they're up or down. They look like they may be wind catchers, but in windy conditions you'll want your rudder in the water anyway. Some upright rudders can be removed and stored in a hatch during transport, which reduces their damage vulnerability. Of more critical importance is the cable and linkage system whereby your feet control the rudder; you want a system where lines and cables won't foul, rudder action is pos-

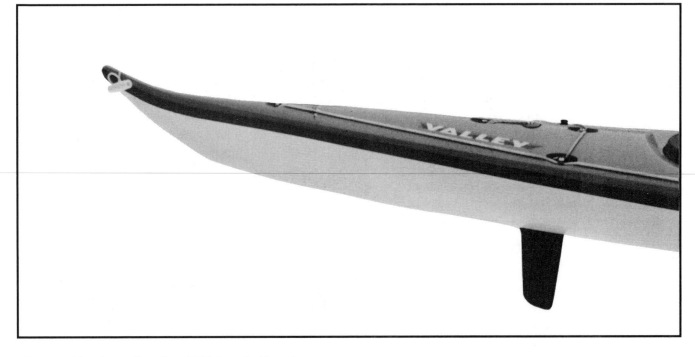

Retractable skeg offered on British-styled kayaks

itive (we describe it as "lack of play" in car steering wheels), and the foot pegs are solid to push against. In the end, keeping the foot-slider and cable-and-rudder assemblies free of sand and grit may be more important than their design, regardless of their elegance or lack thereof.

A skeg is a small fin that is raised and lowered (like a sailboat's center board) in a slot on the underside of the rear hull section. Some British kayaks employ the skeg, on the plausible theory that the rudder is used less for steering than to prevent "weathercocking," which is the tendency of a kayak to turn into the wind, especially frustrating when your desired line of travel is, say, 20 degrees off the wind at your back. The skeg simply gets dropped when wind and waves begin to shove you markedly off course; any minor course

corrections are made by boat leans and paddle strokes (to be described later). If you do acquire a kayak with a skeg, it must be retractable. In certain wind conditions, the extended skeg, which was so helpful in preventing weathercocking, may anchor your stern section so securely that you will have extreme difficulty in turning your bow back up into the wind.

Flush or retractable rudder. Requires two lines to operate.

Nonretractable or upright rudder

Hatches and Bulkheads

Most new kayaks are sold with front and rear bulkheads. If they are watertight, you'll have flotation chambers. Even leaky hatches will take a long time to sap your kayak's buoyancy. If you have gear in waterproof bags in the hatches and cockpit, trapped air in the bags provides flotation as well. If your kayak has no bulkheads (or perhaps no front bulkhead) or if their watertightness is questionable, you must employ inflatable float bags (they come in all sizes and shapes). If they go in through the cockpit, be certain they are tied in or otherwise secured. There are also waterproof gear bags that inflate.

At first glance, bulkheads seem like a "must have" feature. Not necessarily. Bulkheads somewhat limit your flexibility in packing and add weight. A common option is a rear bulkhead but no forward bulkhead. This permits loading of larger gear bags right through the cockpit. Often a small screw hatch is installed in the front deck that allows you to manipulate gear bags as you load and unload through the cockpit. You should consider a rear bulkhead as a basic necessity for safety reasons: it is very difficult to rescue a boat that is flooding at both ends.

The number and variety of hatch systems would take a chapter in itself. In general, the watertight integrity of a hatch is inversely proportional to its size (that is, smaller is drier). Be sure to examine, and even test, large hatches, because only the most well-executed designs are watertight. Most folks prefer larger hatches for easy loading and unloading, so put *all* your gear in waterproof bags; if water gets into a hatch for any reason, your gear is dry. Safety is a consideration, too. We'll discuss matters of safety and rescue in more detail elewhere, but keep in mind that in a kayak with two bulkheads, if the front bulkhead is positioned closer to the footpegs and

the rear one is closer to the rear of the seat, you'll lose cockpit storage but increase your buoyancy and security.

No matter how many float bags, or how watertight your compartments, it's the cockpit that dominates the volumetric capacity of your kayak. In other words, if your cockpit is flooded, you're swamped. In recognition of this, there are kayak designs that employ a "pod" system that limits the amount of water that can flood the cockpit. Also, you can inquire about a sea sock, a spray skirt in reverse, which accomplishes the same thing. The pod or sock are options for those who expect the worst, or plan to go looking for it.

The foregoing discussion assumes that you are always loading up with gear. If you're interested only in day trips and the occasional overnighter, you may be just as happy (and your pocketbook fatter) forgetting about hatches altogether.

Deck Rigging

You can probably get by with simple toggles or straps at each end of the kayak to assist in short carries and as attachment points for bow and stern lines. Safety at sea calls for deck lines, usually running bow to stern, or other straps, which can be grabbed by a thrown rider in a rescue situation. A bowline is a wise accessory, readily accessible for tying up on the beach or landing. A number of hatches employ strap-over-hatch systems, sometimes doubling as a place to stuff an odd-size gear item (a sail mast, for example) or as a place to park your paddle while you squint through your binoculars. Many kayaks are laced with elastic cords fore and aft of the cockpit. The forward ones become a map holder, and a place to jam any other flotsam in search of a home; the rear one may be set up to accommodate a paddle

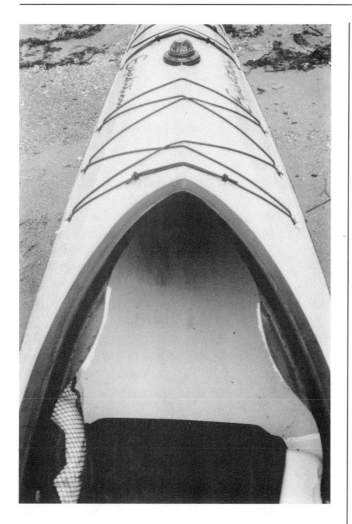

Deck lines fore (shown) and aft of cockpit for map and paddle float, respectively. Note lines running full length of hull for safety. Also, bungie just ahead of deck compass for "paddle park."

float rescue system. (The latter is described in Chapter 5.)

If you happen to find yourself with a kayak all covered with lines, straps, and bungies, resist the urge to use them like the luggage rack on the family station wagon. Deck clutter can exacerbate the effects of wind, deflect waves into your face, and interfere with paddle strokes—or, your prize flotsam may slip off into the deep at the very moment when paddling conditions demand your full attention.

WHAT KAYAKS ARE MADE OF

The three principal materials used for making modern kayaks are fiberglass, polyethylene (plastic), and fabric. A few boats are made of wood (both strip-built and plywood). It's easy to be overwhelmed by materials technology, and the manufacturers themselves engage in a fair amount of mumbo jumbo, so you are often reduced to relying on the reputations of the builder and your dealer. The market is still specialized enough that you can't go too far wrong, in any event. That is, the market is not so large and lucrative that producers of wastebaskets are diverting production capacity to kayaks.

Fiberglass

At this writing, the largest variety of shapes, sizes, and models of touring and sea kayaks is produced in fiberglass. These are essentially custom-built boats, and their weight and cost, as with bicycles, tend to be inversely related. Kevlar is often used in high-priced kayaks because of its tear resistance and high strength-to-weight ratio, but many builders have developed other glass-cloth combinations, epoxy-and-resin cocktails, and lay-up methods that result in kayaks that are both tough and light. Think carefully about paying a premium for an ultralight boat. Only 25 percent of a boat's weight is in the hull (the rest being hatches, hardware, coaming, and so on), and the five or six pounds of weight saved may be at the expense of some hull stiffness or abrasion resistance (especially if the builder leaves off the outer gel coat). Besides weight, you should concern yourself with the quality of the seams, the end pour (at bow and stern), extra thickness of material at abrasion points fore and aft, uniformity of the outer (gel coat) surface, and the smoothness of the inside surfaces. Run your hand around the cockpit rims and the hatch openings to see if they've been sanded smooth.

Consider hull stiffness. A good kayak will have a stiff deck and hull without being too heavy. Several options are available to the builder to achieve stiffness: he can use more expensive materials or a clever blend in his lay-up; the hull and deck shape can be manipulated (an arched hull will be stiffer than a flat-bottomed one); he can use more resin and a thicker gel coat; he may employ internal supports (like a foam pillar, or wood core, or ribs). Some of these methods may add weight out of proportion to the benefit. In the final analysis you will be relying on dealer and builder integrity, but the decision you make is bound to involve considerations of weight, durability, and cost.

Polyethylene

This is as close to mass production as we get in kayak making. Melted poly pellets are either rotationally or blow-molded in coffin-like molds. Plastic boats are slightly heavier than fiberglass boats of equivalent size, and it is difficult to achieve the same sharp entry and fine lines seen in fiberglass boats. Nevertheless, improved technology and new designs have brought more variety and better quality to the plastic boats. There are a number of models so nicely finished that you'll have a hard time identifying them as plastic except upon close examination. Many of the designs are derived directly from boats originally produced in glass, and the small weight penalty is offset by tremendous durability. You can run these babies up on a hundred rocky beaches and suffer only cosmetic scuffs.

Take a close look at the plastic boats and poke and prod them. Linear polyethylene, the most common plastic used in touring kayaks is a non-

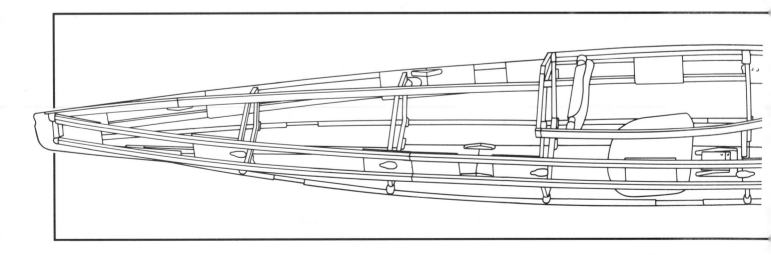

rigid material and must be either formed or internally supported to keep its shape (and stiffness). The larger the boat, the more support is required. A recent development in plastic boat manufacture is a skin foam sandwich that imparts both rigidity and floatation to the hull. But the real story is in the price difference. A plastic boat can save you almost half the price of a fiberglass boat.

Fabric

There are several very high-quality folding boats on the market that employ fabric decks and hulls of Hypalon or other heavy-duty coated fabrics. If you live in an apartment with limited space or if you plan to transport your boat by air, these ingenious and capable craft are worth considering. Because of their internal frame systems, you will give up some storage space. Also, floatation must be provided, and the boats are not light. A good folding boat, as you may have guessed, is expensive. They pack down into one or two duffels, can be assembled in less than half an hour (after you've practiced a few times), and they are equal to the challenge of virtually any ocean

condition. Klepper folding kayaks, which perhaps set the standard for the breed, have crossed open oceans and rounded all the capes. Some sleeker designs, such as the Feathercraft, give up virtually nothing in the way of comfort and performance compared to hard-shelled kayaks.

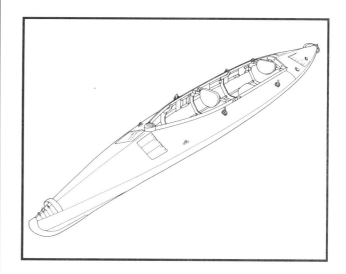

Fabric/collapsible kayak

Collapsible kayak frame

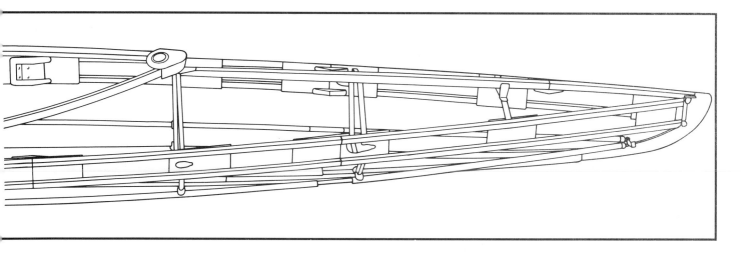

CHAPTER **3**

WHAT YOU'LL NEED
(Besides a Boat)

This sport is relatively inexpensive since the water (or, rather, the use of it) is free and, once you're under way, it's hard to spend much. There are no moorage fees and your kayak can be powered by oatmeal. Compared to virtually any other water sport, save skinny-dipping, it's an incredible bargain.

That's true, but consider the reality. You will need more than just a boat, and most items need to be acquired at the same time as the boat. Your best first step—even before investing a single dollar in hardware—will be to take a lesson, or several. Check around your city or region for either commercial or club programs that provide introductory courses in kayaking. It is very common for retailers who sell paddlesports equipment to offer instruction programs as well. At the very least, they will certainly know where to find instruction. There is a good likelihood that a few hours of instruction will also introduce you to boat designs and other equipment, and thus help guide your hardware decisions and prevent a costly purchasing error.

BEFORE YOU LEAVE THE STORE

Your biggest investment besides the boat could be a good rack. Lots of canoes and kayaks have been hauled lots of miles on two-by-fours on top of rain-gutter clamps. Glue some old shag carpeting to the tops of those stringers to minimize hull abuse and noise. That may work for a canoe resting on its gunwales, but it's bad medicine for kayaks. If you've sunk a thousand dollars—or more—into a new sea kayak and you want to be

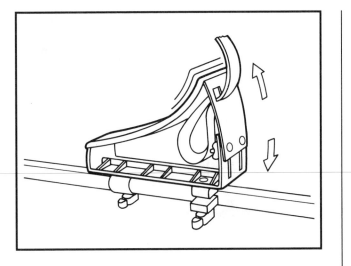

Cradles protect the hull from deforming.

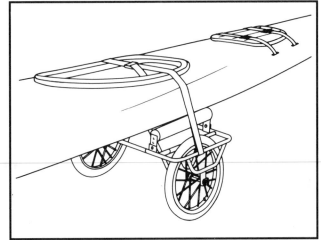

Sturdy wheels make it possible to transport a fully loaded kayak.

confident that your boat will be both secure and protected from abrasion and deformation, get a rack with cradles. Cradles prevent the kayak from shifting from side to side, and they distribute the weight and the tie-down pressure, which can crease or crack the hull.

Both Yakima and Thule make a dazzling array of rack systems, including ones that will go on a rain-gutterless vehicle. Nylon cradles without rubber padding allow you to slide boats on and off from the rear of the vehicle, which is especially helpful for one-person loading or for larger kayaks. Rubber padding on the cradles isn't so good for sliding boats but provides good cushioning and hull protection. It also makes them incredibly secure. I once arrived home after an hour of freeway driving (over 60 MPH) to discover that I had absentmindedly forgotten to put my straps over my boat. It hadn't budged! Rope will work but straps with a cam buckle on one end are prefer-

able. You can do a double loop around your kayak and pull the strap through the one-way teeth of a cam buckle for a bombproof attachment. In a lifetime of boat hauling, I've seen enough of my boats go flying off my car and boat trailer (including one borrowed sea kayak that I never saw again) to believe that a belt, suspenders, and another belt is never too much. One of those belts should always be a bowline.

If you are going to do a lot of kayaking, you may want a method of transport between car and water. In Chapter 4 we discuss a variety of boat-carrying methods, but let's face it: long transports, especially with a loaded boat, are best done with a set of wheels. There are half a dozen models available; some are compact enough to carry in or on your kayak; a few big ones will carry a fully loaded double. In many sea kayaking areas, ferryboats are a popular method of access and egress, and wheels are almost a necessity.

Guidebooks

Do yourself a huge favor and spend ten bucks on a guidebook to canoeable and kayakable waterways in your state or region. Unless you live in eastern Nevada, retailers always carry them. A good guidebook should provide a mix of trips from simple, one-day novice cruises to multi-day expeditions. The trips are usually rated and arranged by degree of difficulty. Perhaps the most important information contained in guidebooks is the whereabouts of launch sites. The only thing worse than not being able to locate a protected launching (and landing) site is to have an angry landowner coming after you with a shotgun—and it gives the sport a bad name. In addition to geography and logistics, a well-researched guidebook will often provide some safety information pertinent to the locale, special hazards, and other sources of maps and weather and marine data.

PADDLE BASICS

The Aleuts sometimes plied the oceans with a single-bladed stick—some might call it a canoe paddle—whose "blade" was simply a flat spot on one end. So, like much else in this sport, we've taken something simple and made it complicated. Today's kayaker has a bewildering choice of paddle sizes, blade shapes, materials, and even colors. One well-regarded paddle maker boasted to me that his company offers, at least theoretically, over 60,000 different combinations! My own collection of paddles is proof that I myself am no slave to simplicity.

Paddle length is a subject on its own, though one wag I know maintains that a paddle only needs to be long enough to reach the water. But if you paddle a wide boat, you may need a longer paddle so that the blades will clear the sides of the hull. A shorter paddle could be satisfactory if the blades were shorter and if the ratio of shaft to blade length were higher. But even when you are satisfied that you've found a paddle long enough so that the blades clear the hull, there are still other considerations.

Think about the paddle as an extension of your arms and as the second part of your transmission system (your legs and foot pegs are the first part). Paddles may be compared to bicycle gears: high gears require big muscles, but once you get up to cruising speed, fewer strokes deliver superior leverage and propulsion. Some people like the feel of a long paddle and the leverage and bracing power it gives them. Low gears and short paddles, on the other hand, require less power but a lot more motion. You can go aerobic with a short paddle; with a long paddle and slow stroke your muscles may give out before your heart rate gets up.

It's a matter of personal preference, but the trend is toward shorter paddles and smaller blades. This makes sense even if you only consider one criterion: the smaller paddle is likely to be lighter. Even a short trip might require up to 5,000 paddle strokes; just 2 ounces can make a huge difference in how you feel at the end of the day—or the next morning.

So what have you got now? Try to avoid paddles weighing more than 2½ pounds, and if you can afford the best, go for one that's less; most popular paddles weigh in at about 2¼ pounds. Be aware of "swing" weight, too; it's critical. If too much of the weight is concentrated in the blade, a 2-pound paddle may feel awkward compared to a heavier one that's better balanced. If you paddle a narrow boat (less than 23 inches at the beam) and you are less than 5 feet 3 inches tall, go for a paddle that's about 210–220 cm long (kayak paddles are sized in centimetres). Scale up from there if you are taller and as your kayak increases in width; this might result in a paddle as long as 250–260 cm for a double kayak. Don't buy a paddle so long that you'll weary of swinging it after twenty minutes, or one so short that you have to lean from side to side just to reach the water. Finally, consider the difference between a delicate and a tough paddle. The touring or wilderness paddler is often pushing off of rough and rocky beaches.

Blade Size and Shape

One look at the assortment of paddle configurations available and you may wish kayakers were still using flattened sticks. The most popular blades are asymmetrical and spooned, but with wide variations in surface area and length. The asymmetrical design results in both the top and bottom of the blade entering the water simultaneously, and a spooned blade grabs more water and flutters less than a flat blade. These blades

Sometimes paddle choice is just a matter of aesthetics.

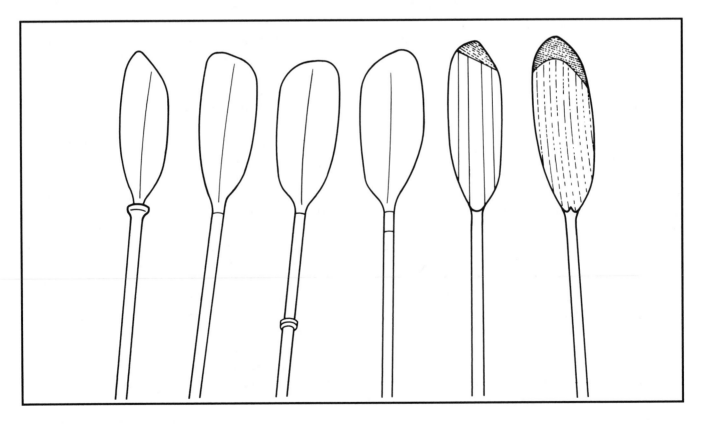

tend to be "self-aligning" in the water, so that you can relax your grip on the paddle. Quite a number of the synthetic paddles also employ a dihedral on the power surface. Here's how the paddle designers explain the advantage of this design: the water is split and released evenly over both sides of the blade as you pull, resulting in less blade flutter while focusing energy toward the shaft. We'll have to take their word for it.

Blade size must be considered, too. A bigger surface area, or "bite," is satisfying to many paddlers and they like the bracing leverage that it gives them. However, just as there has been a trend toward shorter, high-RPM paddles, there has likewise been a move toward smaller blades. The "big bite" theory works for maybe half a dozen strokes, as you accelerate a kayak from a standing start up to cruising speed. Once underway, however you can maintain speed and momentum with a paddle shaft alone. So a new school of thought says go with the very skinny blades (just like what the Eskimos used!). Over long distances there will be less strain on muscles and tendons, though you'll have to live with a slightly compromised brace and Eskimo roll. As for accelerating from a standing start, unless you're a racer, who cares?

One recent and truly revolutionary development in paddles may, nevertheless, be worth describing. That's the wing paddle. The wing was introduced to the world in Olympic flatwater sprint racing, and it did to kayak times what the "bullhorn" handlebars did for bicycle time trials. The wing blade is just that: a "waterfoil" (like an airfoil) that forces a correct stroke and creates lift, which results in the paddle exiting the water *ahead of where it went in.* (A well-executed stroke, regardless of paddle type, is one in which you "plant" the blade and pull the boat up to the blade.) When the wing paddle was first introduced, the experts said it was definitely an advantage to rac-

ers, but of limited utility to recreational paddlers. Now, some new experts claim that rec paddlers can get even more benefit than racers. Early criticism that the wing was ineffective for back paddling, bracing, sculling, and rolling are countered by the claim that all these strokes can be performed; they simply must be learned by practicing and perfecting them with the wing.

Sounds like a good debate, but remember the Aleuts. If you have an opportunity to try one, do it; you might like the wing paddle. But they are costly and not practical as tent poles, digging tools, filet boards, or a lot of other unexpected uses to which paddles get put.

Feathered Versus Unfeathered

Feathered blades orient the blades at an angle to each other so that the recovering blade is "feathered" to the wind during the forward stroke. Unfeathered blades are both on the same plane. You can choose a blade feathered at any angle, up to 90 degrees; 60 degrees is a popular choice. With a feather of less than 90 degrees, you get the benefit of a feathered blade in the wind, while lessening the amount of wrist torque on your control hand (more on this in Chapter 4). The greater the degree of feather, the more the wrist must flex, and that twisting over thousands of strokes has been blamed for causing tendinitis (like tennis elbow) in paddlers. It is often the reason that kayakers choose unfeathered blades. First-time paddlers sometimes choose an unfeathered blade on the rationale that blade orientation and control hand are one less thing to worry about. Another argument for unfeathered blades is also related to the wind. In high winds that hit you from the side, the feathered blade is, in fact, a wind catcher. Paddlers have been knocked over by winds catching their raised paddle blades, or so I'm told.

If you decide to go with feathered blades, you'll have another choice to make: Right or left? This has nothing to do with right- or left-handedness. Unfortunately, virtually every paddlesports retailer and kayak rental operation in America stocks a preponderance of right-hand-control paddles. How do you know which you are? Here's one way to find out. Grab a canoe paddle and take a few strokes. Which side seems more natural to you? If it's left, you will be more comfortable with a left-hand-control kayak paddle.

Fortunately, the only thing more common than right-hand-control paddles are two-piece paddles that allow you to set up for either left, right, *or* unfeathered. It's a good idea to buy one of these first. Two-piece paddles are commonly afflicted with a wobbly connection after regular use, and this is why most kayakers prefer paddling with a one-piece paddle. But you can try a two-piece in all three configurations (right, left, and unfeathered) until you settle on the most comfortable for you. Then buy a one-piece to your liking and the two-piece paddle will become your spare.

Paddle Construction and Materials

My favorite touring paddles are wood, possibly an aesthetic bias. Some of these have a fiberglass layer on the blades, so that a thinner, lighter lamination is possible without sacrificing durability. Wood paddles, because of their flex, may indeed be kinder and gentler on the joints and tendons of the long-distance paddler. But if you find that you have to scratch half a pound in weight, you might be better off with a lighter paddle of synthetic materials. Very good synthetic paddles, reasonably light, feature a pressure-molded fiber-

glass shaft with thin fiberglass blades. Such a paddle might retail for $150; and prices will increase as the composites become more exotic and the weight decreases (like a bike), until you max out at $300 for a graphite composite. Add an additional premium for wing blades.

My final thought on paddles is that they are a personal thing, an extension, quite literally, of *you;* so get one that is aesthetically pleasing and lightweight. A heavy, clunky paddle sabotages the kayaking experience. This is the place to splurge.

SAFETY ACCESSORIES

Spray Skirt

In Chapter 2, we discussed cockpit shapes and sizes. Regardless of cockpit size, you want a spray skirt that fits securely around the cockpit rim—but is not so taut that it won't release easily in an emergency—and which you can pull up under your armpits to keep water out of your lap. Indeed, a spray skirt is not an option, but a necessity that transforms a delicate little boat with no freeboard into a seaworthy kayak. They come in a variety of styles, each with their special advantages and disadvantages. All-nylon spray skirts are inexpensive and dry quickly, but they make an infernal crackling sound as you paddle, and they need suspenders to keep them up. Neoprene skirts fit snugly around your trunk, provide a drum-tight deck, are warm and quiet, but are always soggy. A good compromise are skirts that have neoprene decks and nylon uppers.

Except on a warm sunny day on quiet and protected waters, you should always wear a spray skirt. Its minimum function is to keep the water that seesaws back and forth on your paddle shaft from drooling into your lap. It won't be a 20-foot rogue wave but the wake from a boat on your local lake suddenly washing over your deck and filling your cockpit that will make a believer out of you.

Personal Floatation Devices (PFDs)

Once called "life preservers," you need a Type III PFD that bears the approval of the United States Coast Guard. A popular style of PFD, known as a "shorty," works well for the kayaker. Longer-waisted PFDs will give you additional floatation, but make sure the bottom cuff can be rolled up. You want a short PFD, one that doesn't push down or interfere with the deck of your spray skirt. It should also have wide and comfortable arm-holes and be snug enough that it doesn't ride up when you're afloat, but it should not be so tight as to restrict movement. Type III PFDs must be able to support 15½ pounds (most adults weigh between 10 and 12 pounds in the water). Most good-quality recreational PFDs provide floatation well in excess of that. It is not a sure thing that a PFD will float an unconscious person face-up, so you should test yours in the water to see if you can relax with your head back and your chin above water. If you cannot, you may need a different sort of PFD or one with a higher floatation rating. A good PFD is a colorful accessory, a warm, insulating layer, a backrest, and, yes, a lifesaver. While on the water, wear it outside, not under a paddling or rain jacket. There have been reports of paddling jackets or anoraks being ballooned out by the PFD—filling with water and largely canceling the floatation of the PFD.

Paddle Float

If your kayak does not have rigging for inserting a paddle blade behind the cockpit, you should have some installed if you plan to venture beyond the most benign waters. The most commonly taught and easily mastered self-rescue is done with a paddle float (see Chapter 5), and it works best if you have a way to secure the paddle to the kayak deck, the rigging, and a float. The float can be an old Clorox bottle (8 pounds of floatation), a kayak seat cushion, or an inflatable bag made specifically for rescue (40 pounds of floatation). The latter are quickly inflated (or may be inflated before embarkation), and slipped over the other end of the paddle to create the outrigger that will allow you to reenter a swamped kayak. An alternative to the paddle float is a set of inflatable sponsons. These are pictured and described in Chapter 5.

Bilge Pump

Back in your swamped kayak, you'll need to get the water out of the cockpit. Some British kayaks have lever-action bilge pumps built right into the hull; absent that, you can purchase a relatively inexpensive portable one that can move a lot of water quickly.

Sponge

A sponge won't empty a swamped kayak, but you'll want one to remove the puddle that inevitably forms in your cockpit from leaky water jugs, dripping paddles, dripping boots, rain, or a pinhole leak in the hull.

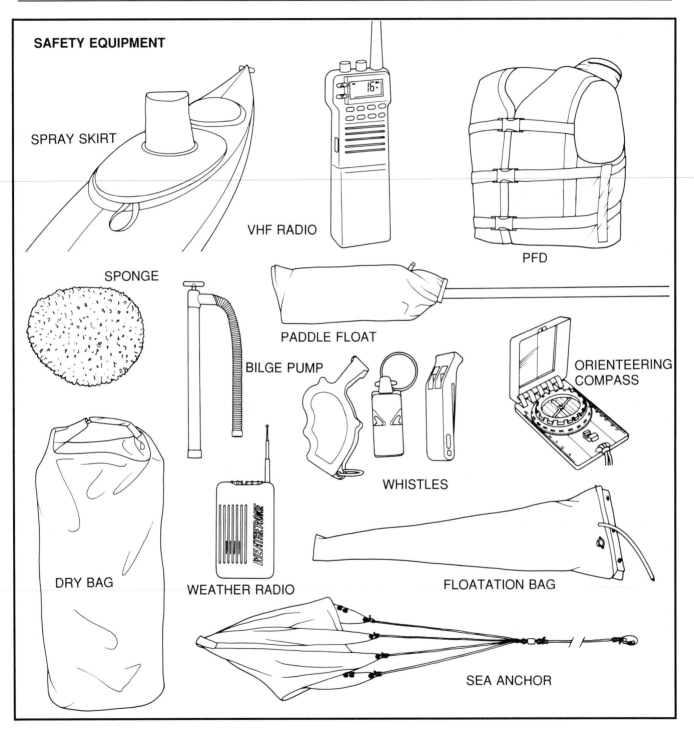

SAFETY EQUIPMENT

SPRAY SKIRT

VHF RADIO

PFD

SPONGE

PADDLE FLOAT

BILGE PUMP

ORIENTEERING COMPASS

WHISTLES

DRY BAG

WEATHER RADIO

FLOATATION BAG

SEA ANCHOR

Weather Radio

An inexpensive VHF radio pretuned to the national weather network (of the National and Atmospheric Administration—the NOAA) is a good accessory whether you are a sea kayaker, back country skier, or just planning a picnic. Whether you tune in on the morning of your planned day trip or carry your radio on an extended trip, the NOAA marine forecast (or the Canadian equivalent) should be your first line of preparedness. Knowing when to stay off the water is worth more than all the other accessories for safety combined.

Sea Anchor

If you need a sea anchor, you probably don't need to be reading this book. I, in fact, carry one—not because I plan to cross the North Sea, but because they're useful for holding the boat in place when I go bottom fishing in even a light breeze. It's an underwater parachute that opens when you throw it overboard; your kayak aligns with the wind direction and, *in extremis,* that's how you avoid broaching in violent seas. You are, of course, still subject to the currents, whether wind- or tide-driven, but you move in concert, not in opposition, to them.

Dry Bags

These are not a safety item *per se,* but if your only warm clothing is getting soaked in a not-so-dry hatch, or in your cockpit, and the temperature drops and the winds begin to whistle, you will indeed be at risk. Even if your dry bags are stuffed with clothes—even cookware and canned foods —they add floatation to your kayak. Dry bags in

several sizes, and perhaps a rigid container for sensitive items like camera or binoculars, are important accessories no matter how tame the destination.

And that brings us to the crux of the matter.

DRESSING FOR SUCCESS (IN THE WET)

You don't have to be an old salt to understand that this sport is wet. And if it's wet, it has the potential to be cold, even in a warm, dry climate. Camped out in a 100-degree desert, given a gallon of water and a towel during mid-day, I can cool a bottle of wine down to 40 degrees for you. That's a great trick for wine, but for people, exposure to wind and wet can progress quickly to a life-threatening situation. Hypothermia may result in the body's core temperature dropping to 80 degrees, at which point death is likely. At a few degrees below the body's normal 98.6 temperature, you can only be revived by an external source of warmth. Hypothermia and exposure are a threat anywhere on the water, but three of our most popular sea kayaking areas—the North Atlantic coast, the Pacific coast, and the Great Lakes— have waters typically under 50 degrees. A swim in mid-forties water will reduce you to numb ineffectiveness in about fifteen minutes.

That sounds like a case for wet suits and dry suits, which are routinely worn by whitewater paddlers, and they can be worn by sea kayakers if extreme conditions and very cold waters are anticipated. But unless you are planning on doing Eskimo rolls or other heroics (or perhaps drills), you might better spend your time and money on refining your skills. Wet suits and dry suits are hot, uncomfortable, and restrictive for the kayak tourer, who will be stroking continuously. After a

DRESSING FOR SUCCESS

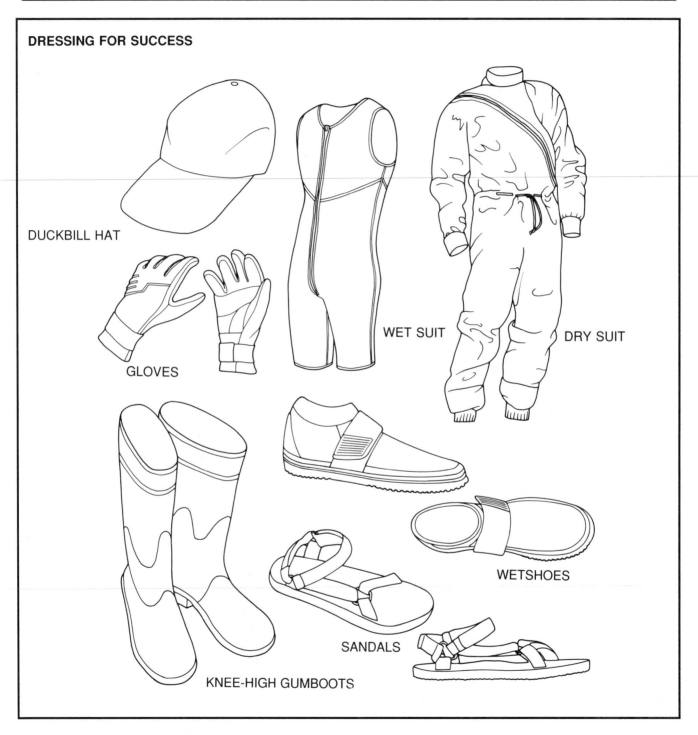

DUCKBILL HAT

GLOVES

WET SUIT

DRY SUIT

WETSHOES

SANDALS

KNEE-HIGH GUMBOOTS

Author in full regalia: Patagonia anorak with hood, draw waist, and neoprene wrist cuffs; shorty PFD and heavy-duty, all-neoprene sprayskirt; foul-weather pants with bib top (under anorak). Note drip rings on paddle shaft. Kayak has deck lines, deck-mounted compass, and "hip clips" in cockpit.

ture. The layers insulate you and can be shed as temperatures rise. Even when the air temperatures are in the low fifties, when breezes are 10 to 15 MPH, and 45-degree water is splashing over me, I may be wearing no more than a water-repellent anorak over a long-sleeved polypropylene undershirt. The spray skirt tunnel is pulled up under my armpits, the anorak is over the skirt, and my PFD is over my anorak. After a few hundred strokes, I am very warm, indeed. Most heat loss is through the head, so a fleece or wool hat is your best cold-weather defense. A broad-brimmed hat or even a traditional Sou'wester is a must for paddling in the rain.

In warm, dry weather you can keep stripping down until you're in your bathing suit. But keep that polypro shirt, your hat, and a paddle jacket handy. In a few moments' time, a cloud can obscure the sun, and even a light breeze speeding the evaporation of paddle splash off your body or T-shirt can cool you down like my desert wine bottle. A combination that will work in most weather conditions is a short-sleeved, water-repellent, nylon paddling pullover (they weigh only a few ounces) on top of a long-sleeved polypro undershirt. Your rain suit top or anorak should be at the ready if the weather deteriorates.

Below the deck is less critical. You can paddle in a pair of shorts, worn under rain pants, in any kind of weather. Warmth isn't usually a problem when you're spray-skirted in a cozy cockpit and protected from evaporative cooling and wind chill; the main objective is just to keep the dripping water off your legs and out of your lap.

In cold water and in wet, cold weather the only thing more in need of cover than your head is your hands. Treat yourself to paddlers' mitts, or "pogies," which come in neoprene or pile-lined nylon and which attach right to your paddle shaft. You have a bare-handed grip on your paddle shaft but your paws stay warm and relatively dry.

day or two they also begin to smell like dead fish.

In cold weather, wear a water-repellent paddling jacket or anorak over a synthetic shirt and/or pile sweater. Synthetics and pile are hydrophobic (they hate water) and keep you from getting that "clammy" feeling. Wool is effective, too, but avoid cotton garments, which hold their mois-

It's also a defense against "prune hands" resulting from the water that seesaws along your paddle. Serious paddlers shouldn't leave shore without paddling gloves or mitts. Hands disabled due to cold put you at risk.

Finally, but critically, you need something on your feet. If your paddling waters are uniformly warm, sandals, old sneakers, or mesh "aqua socks" are fine; otherwise, knee-high gum boots are inexpensive and effective. With them you can wade in deep enough to enter your boat afloat; you can jump out on a beach and land your boat; you can clamber over a rocky landing, trudge through the gravel, and usually keep your feet dry. If you do happen to fill a boot, it can be dried out quickly. Neoprene wetsuit booties seem like a good idea but have definite drawbacks; they're perpetually wet—and therefore cold—and they hold their odor like a grudge. If you do choose neoprene booties, wear a polypro or wool sock inside. These can be washed and dried to overcome bootie breath.

CHAPTER **4**

A QUICK START
(On Quiet Water)

Despite the mystique that surrounds sea kayaking, few recreational vehicles are easier to master. This may beg the question of whether the ability to swim is a necessary prerequisite to kayaking. Objectively, the answer is no. Swimmers and nonswimmers alike should always wear a PFD, and it is a rare circumstance indeed when you would willingly let go of your kayak. We earlier pointed out that a properly constructed and/or outfitted kayak should float indefinitely. Swimming is likely the last thing you'd want to do; it saps energy and increases the chance of hypothermia. That's the objective analysis. Practically speaking, however, persons who know how to swim and are comfortable around the water are less likely to panic in the event of a capsize.

When the beginning skier faces his first steep, icy descent, or the tyro biker is faced with honking traffic, barking dogs or a steep, twisting downhill,

the game changes. Knowledge and experience are what count. When the kayaker finds himself far from shore, in dense fog, or beset by powerful winds, and a passing ferryboat sends a 4-foot wave over his bow, he'll need more than this chapter to bring himself home.

But even a thousand-mile journey begins with a first step (goes an ancient proverb). Now is the time to get in and go. Warm, shallow water, protected from the wind and devoid of motorized traffic, is a good place to start. Wear clothing and footwear suitable for wading and getting wet.

FROM CAR TO WATER

At some point you have to carry your boat. For a very short carry you can simply pick up the boat by the cockpit and walk it to the water on your thighs. The next level of "schlepping" is to do a one-armed press and rest the kayak on a shoulder, with a PFD for padding. Irreverent owners of plastic kayaks may just drag their boats, Christopher Robin–style, over any and all terrain. It works, but don't tell anyone you read it here. If you are kayaking with a friend, the answer is simple. Each of you takes an end of either one or both kayaks.

BOAT ENTRY

Launchings and landings have the highest potential for getting you wet, and this soaking will likely be witnessed by large numbers of people. So, if you do nothing else, perfect these moves!

There are two basic ways to get into the boat: off a dock or embankment, and on a beach. In either case, check the surroundings. A boat wake can arrive from across the bay and create havoc with your embarkation. Set your foot pegs or rudder controls for your height *before* you put the boat in the water. And pull your spray skirt on.

For a launch parallel to a low dock or bank, set the kayak into the water and place one end of the paddle shaft on the back deck of your kayak just behind the cockpit with the other end of the paddle shaft resting on the shore or dock. Put the paddle blade flat on the shore or dock; the other blade extends beyond the kayak deck. You can now sit or crouch on the dock or shore in front of the paddle shaft. Reach back and place one hand

With your paddle blade on the beach or dock and the shaft behind your cockpit, lower yourself into the cockpit.

Your elbows should form a right angle.

GRIP

To determine proper arm-to-paddle geometry, extend your arms in front of yourself, keeping your elbows straight.

on the paddle shaft behind the cockpit. Grab both the shaft and the cockpit rim; the other hand is on the shaft extending toward the shore or dock. Make sure you can raise and lower your body weight supported on the deck and paddle shaft; then, put your legs, one at a time, into the cockpit. Keep your weight on the paddle shaft and your grip on the cockpit. Don't try to stand in the kayak. Now, simply lower yourself into the seat. In some of the very large cockpits you can sit down first and then extend the legs. More likely, however, you'll have to extend your legs into the cockpit first as you lower yourself. If this sounds too complicated (it isn't), you can practice a few entrances on your front lawn first. To get out of the kayak, simply reverse the process: with paddle shaft on dock and deck, grab the shaft with two hands (one on cockpit rim) and raise your butt out of the kayak.

The same paddle-shaft support method can be used when launching off a beach with all or just the bow of the kayak in the water. Lower yourself into the kayak while it sits mostly or completely on a sandy or pebbly beach. Once in the cockpit, snap the spray skirt around the rim and use your hands—or one hand and the paddle—to push yourself into the water. This works best in an empty kayak with a gently sloping beach and is also the launch of choice into breaking surf when there's no time for attaching the spray skirt before the first wave lands in your lap. Using the paddle as a push pole is common. Consider this when you buy your paddle: pushing off can be risky, especially with lightweight models.

AFLOAT!

Now you're launched. Attach the back of your spray skirt along the back of the cockpit rim and pull the front over the cockpit nose; then snap the sides under the cockpit rim. You should have already adjusted your backrest—firm back support is important—and foot pegs so that you are firmly in the saddle. That means you can push solidly on the foot pedals (or rudder controls), and that your knees are forced gently up against the deck, but not so tightly that you can't drop your knees to relax your hamstrings. Resist the urge to lie back against the deck as if it were a lounge chair. Your legs, butt, and torso are part of the transmission system and are rendered ineffective in the reclining position.

The Grip

Without any instruction you would intuitively put one blade in the water and pull, then the other. The kayak would start moving and you'd be under way. But to increase your range and control you need to learn an efficient stroke. You first need a proper grip and the proper arm-to-paddle geometry. Grab your paddle with both hands and hold the paddle across your chest. Your hands should be just outside your shoulders and an equal distance from each blade. Wrap a couple of strips of electrical tape around your paddle shaft so your hands will "remember" where they belong.

Extend the paddle in front of you a few inches above the deck. Your elbows are straight, *not bent.* If you have chosen an unfeathered paddle, your grip will result in both blades being perpendicular to the water. For a right-hand control paddle, grip the shaft with your right hand so that the right blade is perpendicular to the water (vice versa for left-hand control paddle). Feel the oval of the shaft with your control hand. Your non-control hand should form a loose collar around the shaft so that when you cock up the wrist of your right (or control) hand, the shaft rotates easily through your non-control hand and you bring the left blade perpendicular to the water. You will cock up your control wrist every time you "wind up" for a stroke with the non-control-side blade. With an unfeathered paddle, both hands grip the paddle and only a slight cock of the wrists is necessary to bring the alternating blades perpendicular.

The Stroke

Your paddle is extended in front of you over the deck. Keep your left elbow straight as you pull back the right hand, like a pitcher's windup. Your torso should wind up to the right, too. The object of the game is to plant the left blade as far forward in the water as possible, and to do so with torso rotation and arm extension—not by bending forward. Now, plant the blade and pull the boat to the blade as you "unwind" your torso, and punch out your upper arm. The punching out of your upper arm should also be part of the paddle stroke; use your extended left hand as a fulcrum for applying force to your "lever" (the paddle shaft). Your left arm stays straight throughout the stroke, until you bend it to pick up the blade for the right-side stroke. End your stroke as the paddle blade reaches your hips, and if you really rotated your torso—rather than merely articulating your elbows—your blade comes out of the water still perpendicular to the water and pointed away from the boat.

Here are two good tricks for getting powerful strokes that use your strong back and shoulder muscles, not wimpy arm muscles: first, watch

FORWARD STROKE

To start the basic stroke, rotate your torso to the right, wind up with the right arm, and punch out with the left. (Notice how the hand opens up on the forward hand.) The object of the game is to plant the left paddle blade as far forward as possible.

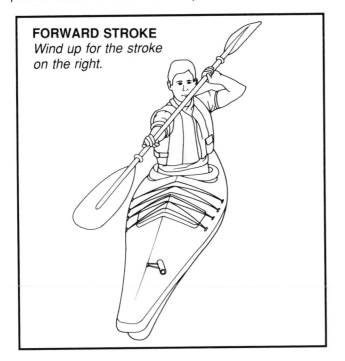

FORWARD STROKE
Wind up for the stroke on the right.

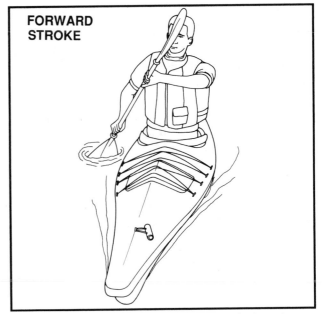

FORWARD STROKE

The punching arm is almost fully extended as the pulling blade begins to exit the water.

your PFD's zipper. It should move from side to side, which indicates that you are rotating your torso. Second, look at your elbow after punching out your arm for the new blade plant. It should be straight. Simply moving the elbows back and forth is a substitute for torso rotation. It works, but it results in a weak stroke and sore elbows.

GOING IN A STRAIGHT LINE

Most touring kayaks, unlike whitewater kayaks, have a straight keel line and V-shaped ends that make the boat *want* to go in a straight line, or to "track." Even if your kayak has a rudder, leave it up for now. A straight line is the shortest distance between two points, and going straight is a worthy goal for a kayak paddler. In the distance of just 50 yards, a number of factors will cause your rudderless kayak to go off course. A more powerful stroke on one side may cause the boat to turn away from that side. A slight breeze may cause the boat to turn into the wind. To keep your kayak on course you have several options.

Let's say the kayak starts veering to the left: just take an extra stroke or two on the left side. Or put more power into your left-side stroke. You could even change your grip to extend the shaft and blade on the left side, resulting in greater leverage. As a last resort, you could quickly drop your right blade into the water as a rudder. As you spend more time on the water, such microadjustments will become second nature and you will also learn the boat-turning techniques (still without a rudder) that are, ironically, part of going in a straight line when wind and waves enter the picture.

TURNING

Most of your time in a sea kayak is spent going in a straight line, but there are critical times when you need to know how to turn the kayak, rudder or no rudder. These occasions are primarily those of getting in and out of tight places, usually while launching or landing, and as an adjunct to going straight when conditions get rough. The most effective kayak turn is accomplished with a stroke and a boat lean.

The turning stroke is called a sweep, and it is executed on the side you are turning away from. In the forward stroke, the paddle blade thrusts parallel to the keel line; for the sweep, you must carve an arc with your blade. Start the sweep by planting the blade as far forward as possible and push the blade outward, sweep it in a broad arc, and finish with a powerful draw of the blade toward the stern of the boat. Blade orientation is

Paddler has cocked boat to the left edge to make the boat turn right.

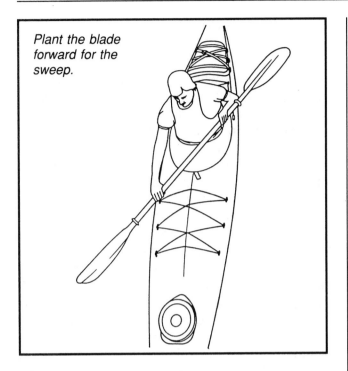

Plant the blade forward for the sweep.

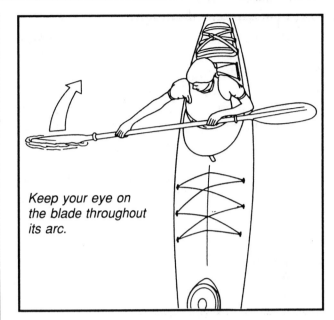

Keep your eye on the blade throughout its arc.

important for the sweep. Twist the blade by rolling your wrist forward slightly so that the blade will sweep water away from the bow. Since most of the turning impetus occurs at the start and the end of the stroke, you will eventually learn to dispense with a full sweep. If you simply twist your body toward the rear of the kayak and plant your paddle blade at the halfway point in the arc between cockpit and stern and draw the stern toward the paddle, you will have a stroke that, in fact, has a name: the stern draw. The key to this, and to virtually every stroke, is to rotate your shoulders and torso so that they follow the blade. Keep your eye on the paddle blade, as if there were a line from your nose to the blade tip.

It may take several sweeps, or stern draws, to turn the boat, and even this may not get you around as fast as you'd like. Cocking the boat over on its edge—that is, to the outside of the turn—is a surefire way to accelerate the turn.

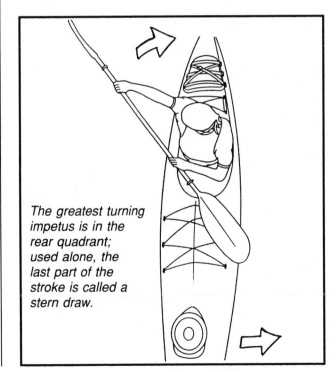

The greatest turning impetus is in the rear quadrant; used alone, the last part of the stroke is called a stern draw.

Lean the boat, not your body, by cocking the boat with your hips. Your objective is to get the keel at bow and stern out of the water. Also, by putting the boat on its edge, or bilges, you create a rounded or "rockered" bottom that turns rather than tracks. If cocking your hips doesn't seem to do it for you, try lifting the inside knee and dropping the outside knee. With practice, you'll become more comfortable about leaning your boat and will develop a fine sense of its limits of stability. (More on this later.)

THE RUDDER

We could have safely assumed that your boat was equipped with a rudder and that turns could be effected simply by pushing on the left pedal to go left, on the right to go right. (A no-brainer!) I happen to think a rudder is an important accessory, and for extended trips I wouldn't be without one. But if your objective is to learn how to control a kayak, you need to learn the techniques and hull characteristics that affect a turn. Rudder failure or jamming is not common, but it's a definite possibility. Rough water conditions may demand a combination of rudder and paddler skill to make the right move. And one day you may find yourself sitting in a rudderless boat—rented, borrowed, or incapacitated—and the excuse that you've never been in one before won't cut it. Even when the rudder works fine, the harder you use it, the more it drags, so good technique combined with a rudder is more efficient.

GOING BACKWARDS

There are times when you will want to back up: when you are moving into a docking or landing position in quiet water or holding back at a landing approach to keep from getting surfed onto or into the beach. Your paddle grip and blade orientation are exactly the same as for the forward stroke, but you use the *back* of the blade—the non-power face—rather than the front. The torso comes into play for the back strokes, too. With your rudder up, start by rotating your upper body to the left, plant the left blade and apply power—pushing down more than out—to the non-power face of the blade by unwinding or rotating around to the right for the right-side blade plant, and so on. In fact, paddling backwards is an excellent drill for developing a feel for torso rotation. Most people can get by with the elbow paddling to make the kayak go forward, but without torso rotation, going backwards becomes a spectacularly clumsy exercise.

GOING SIDEWAYS

The paddle blade control necessary to maneuver a kayak into a parallel parking position at dock or beach side—or, more critically, in a rescue—will, if practiced and perfected, become a major element of boat control if you should ever find yourself in difficult open-water situations. You would serve yourself well by practicing the following strokes, not so you'll be the most elegant kayak docker, but to develop a keen sense of blade angle and of the connection between you, the paddle, and the kayak. The stroke is called a "draw," and the object is to move your kayak sideways.

Sit erect in your cockpit. Rotate your upper body in the direction you wish to move your boat (left, say) so that your PFD zipper points away from your hull by as near to 90 degrees as your flexibility will allow. Your paddle grip is just as it would be to initiate a forward stroke, but as you rotate to the left you'll bring the paddle shaft vertical by pushing your right forearm across your brow so that your right grip is actually over the water. If your rotation is wimpy, you won't be able to get your paddle shaft vertical and your stroke will consist of pushing down on water rather than achieving the goal of pulling the boat to your paddle. If you succeed in a good torso rotation—with your lower arm fully extended over the water, and your upper hand over the water—plant the paddle blade as far out from the hull as possible and pull the boat to the paddle. You will need to get the blade out of the water before it goes under the boat. To do this, drop your upper hand forward onto the deck; it's a lot easier than lifting the paddle up. Try a series of blade plants and pulls to see if you can make your kayak slip sideways. You will have to fine-tune the angle of the blade, by drawing toward either the bow or stern, to get a perfect 90-degree sideslip.

A boat lean can help a turn, but for a sideslip you need a flat boat. Start your blade plant with a slight lean, then flatten the boat. If you find you are tending to lean toward the paddle to get your blade out from the boat, you are simply compensating for insufficient torso rotation.

The official name for this stroke is the "draw." The draw stroke, with a dozen variations, is the most important stroke in a whitewater paddler's repertoire. It's not quite so crucial to sea kayakers, but your time spent perfecting it will not be wasted.

Once you've developed the feel for sideslipping your boat—in either direction—by repeated blade plants, try a "sculling" draw. This will also provide

Rotate your torso; plant the blade well away from the boat. Keep the shaft as vertical as possible; note that the top hand is over the water.

DRAW STROKE

To move sideways, pull your boat to the blade, and get the blade out of the water before it goes under the hull.

you with the ultimate feel for blade control. With your blade planted 90 degrees away from your cockpit, and vertical, try carving a figure eight with your blade, using blade-angle changes to create pressure and a sideslip of the hull. The sensation is much like the lift created—every kid has done this—when you hold your flat hand out of a moving car window and make subtle changes in the plane of your hand. Sculling with your blade allows you to keep slicing the blade away from the hull, on the outside of your figure eight, and you can sideslip indefinitely without taking your paddle out of the water.

LANDING AND EXITING

Landing at a dock, a sloping beach, or a low embankment in quiet water is no great trick, especially if you've mastered a backstroke, a turn, and a sideslip. You sidle up to the beach or dock, unsnap your spray skirt, put your paddle behind you with the shaft on the deck and blade on the dock or bank, and do a reverse push-up on your paddle shaft. Lift your butt out from the cockpit onto the dock or shore, bringing one leg and then the other.

On gently sloping sand or gravel beaches you can also charge the beach, give a powerful stroke, lean back in your cockpit (to lift the bow) and slide your kayak right up on the beach. The beach-charge landing can shorten the life of your kayak, but so long as the beach isn't rocky or barnacled, your boat will suffer only minor abrasion. If there's some wave action—6 inches or more—you can approach steeper beaches at a 45-degree angle. Choose this gambit when there's even a slight surf (see Chapter 9 for strategies and techniques for dealing with heavier surf), and unsnap your skirt before you charge the beach so that you can jump out and pull the boat up before the pursuing waves wash into your cockpit or pull your kayak back into the water. If you've slid far enough up on the beach, you won't need to use your paddle to exit; rest your paddle on the foredeck and shore, do a push-up with your arms on the cockpit rim, and then grab the front of the cockpit to pull yourself up; step out.

Do yourself a favor. Get in the habit of pulling your kayak well up on the beach, and tie it to something solid. Put your paddle and your spray skirt in the cockpit. Or you might want to *tie* your spray skirt to the front grab loop of your kayak to dry. Sudden gusts of wind, rising tides, and rogue waves have all been known to move boats, paddles, and skirts to parts unknown while their oblivious owners were making a too-fast transition to shore activities.

DRILLS

Stop! Don't rush on to the next section. We're an impatient society, but mastery of a few fundamentals can really pay off, especially when you find yourself away from the protected environments where most of your learning should take place. The following moves are simple in concept, but it's amazing how many people are taking risks on open water without having mastered them. Longtime world slalom kayak champion Richard Fox uses an elaborate version of this drill before every workout and race. But, as a river runner, he's never far from shore and doesn't need to jog his muscle memory as much as you do.

Spins

Keep your kayak flat and start sweep strokes on one side. The object is to make a broad arc with your paddle blade, following it with your torso and eyes, to spin your boat 360 degrees using the fewest possible strokes. At the completion of your forward sweep—on the left, say—rotate your shoulders to the right and plant your right blade far back toward the stern of the kayak, like a rudder, and use the non-power face of the blade as you carve a reverse arc from stern to bow. Always follow your blade with your eyes. Your torso should rotate in the direction of both the forward and reverse sweep stroke, which you should link to make a smooth spin. After you have achieved a series of 360-degree spins to the right, reverse the strokes—forward sweep on right and reverse sweep on left—to spin your boat counterclockwise. Touch your paddle to the hull as you start each sweep, forward and reverse; now you know you've rotated enough.

This drill is a lot easier in a short, rocker-bottomed whitewater kayak than in a touring kayak, but the purpose of the exercise is the same: the mastery of blade placement, blade angle, torso rotation, and control of the boat.

Boat Leans

Try cocking your boat up on one edge by lifting one knee (while dropping the other) and paddling three or four strokes on the low side. When the boat starts to veer away from your paddling side (it will!), bring the boat flat and sweep with your paddle on the opposite side; then cock up the boat on the new side and do three or four strokes. Alternate edges, lifting one knee and then the other, and, with the boat flat, take a sweep stroke

to bring the kayak back on course after each "on-edge" sequence. This drill will hone your boat-lean skills as well as your sweep stroke. If you really put your boat on edge, the drill is also likely to result in a capsize in your first attempts, so choose your practice site accordingly: shallow and warm!

Sideslipping

Using either a series of draw strokes or a sculling draw, try moving your kayak sideways 10 to 20 yards at a 90-degree angle to the longitudinal axis of the kayak. Pull your kayak back in the other direction. Keep a flat boat, or if you want to reduce resistance even further, lean the boat slightly away from the direction of the sideslip.

Paddling Backwards

This stroke is described above. With practice, you'll learn to use the back, or non-power, face of your paddle blade and develop a better torso rotation.

Getting Wet and Getting Out

In the next chapter we're going to get into some advanced defensive techniques, but before you try anything else, including these strokes and drills, try just tipping over and getting out of the boat. It's called a "wet exit." The question I'm most often asked by non-kayaking bystanders is, "How do you get out of that thing?" You want to learn this early. There's nothing to it.

Check to make sure you know where your spray skirt grab loop is—and that it is *outside* of the cockpit, not tucked under it. In warm, shallow water, or in a pool, hang on to your paddle with one hand, and throw all your weight to one side to capsize the kayak. If you pull the front of your spray skirt off the cockpit, usually you'll just fall right out of the cockpit. If your kayak has a small cockpit or is outfitted for a snug fit, grab the sides of the cockpit after you've released the spray skirt and push yourself out. Keep hold of your paddle and the kayak as you exit and surface. You don't want either of them to get away from you. After your head is above water, try to wriggle, or throw yourself, up onto the bottom of the hull to reassure yourself that it is a buoyant little island. (For this exercise, the kayak is better off upside down, since air will be trapped in the cockpit and provide even more buoyancy.)

To empty the kayak, keep it upside down; tilt the kayak slightly to expose the cockpit rim; pick up the bow (where most of the water is) and let the stern sink. If there's a bulkhead behind the seat, that's usually all that's needed to get out most of the water.

BIG WATER

You can find ample rewards and lifelong satisfaction paddling the quiet and protected waterways that are all around us. Urban adventures among the wharves and houseboats of a small harbor or poking into the estuaries of small rivers may be as much as you want to tackle. It's reassuring to know that the kayak in which you're gliding among the lily pads of an arboretum is capable of crossing 20 miles of open ocean in 12-foot seas; you can leave the derring-do to others.

For many of us, however, the mastery of skills and the expanding of our expeditionary horizons is a source of real satisfaction. Even if those expeditions, in reality, turn out to be close to home or rated as "protected" in the guidebook, sudden squalls, a forced detour into more difficult water, or some other chance factors can present the paddler with more than he bargained for. Randall Washburne, a recognized authority on sea kay-

aking suggests two lines of defense for paddlers: the first is preparation, equipment, weather forecasting, and the seamanship to keep you out of harm's way.

If, despite careful planning and execution, you do find yourself in adverse conditions, you have a second line of defense: evasive maneuvers, bracing strokes, and self-rescues. Many people tackle open water and coastal voyages without ever mastering the braces or self-rescues. They survive by their knowledge of the seas, navigation, and weather sense (aided, perhaps, by a VHF receiver), and they may be quite successful. Your practice and mastery of these techniques is a matter of personal choice, and perhaps a form of insurance.

EVASIVE MANEUVERS

A good nose for shifts in the weather may be a more effective defense than anything you can do with a boat or paddle (we'll examine the dynamics of the "weather machine" in the following chapter). The first and best evasive maneuver is avoidance, as in "Don't go!"

But you started out on your voyage and now you're on the water. We'll disregard, for the moment, random catastrophe, such as a rogue wave or being mowed down by a drunken power boater (the latter is not farfetched). The most likely turn of events is a sudden squall or a front that threatens either your forward progress or stability with wind and waves. At the first sniff of trouble, make sure that your spray skirt is secure, your PFD is zippered, and your outerwear (anorak, pogies, hat) is equal to a good blow. If there are any loose items tucked under deck bungies, get them below deck.

Your options may be limited, but your first question has to be: Where is the nearest protected shore—a shore out of the wind? Even a tiny islet will break the wind and swell to give you a respite. I've burrowed into many a thicket to hunker down and wait out the blow. If possible, get behind a point of land where you and your boat can get out of the water. Here's a good time to get a fire or stove going. A pot of tea is a more prudent goal than getting back on the water prematurely.

If such protection is not near at hand, you must make some tricky calculations. Pressing on with your present course only makes sense if it is the fastest way to protected water. And "the fastest way" is a relative concept, dependent upon the direction of the wind and the resulting waves. As waves build, the most difficult paddling conditions may be when they are coming from the side (abeam), so you'll want to take that into account.

Running with the Wind

Running with the wind and waves may be a good strategy if it promises a fast way to a landing spot. A crash landing in surf on a sand or gravel beach would be inelegant, at best, or bruising, at worst, but preferable to being capsized far from shore. Running with big waves, however, may find you surfing, and surfing an 18-foot-long sea kayak requires some very advanced boat-handling skills. Also, most kayaks want to turn upwind, and this can make it very difficult for the inexperienced paddler to bring his kayak around to run downwind. Right at the moment of transition from abeam to downwind, you are at the greatest peril. This strategy can be risky.

Quartering

If you are able to make headway, sea kayaks tend to handle best when quartering upwind. *Quartering* refers to a course that is roughly halfway between a line directly into the waves and directly abeam of the waves. A direct frontal attack forces you to climb and descend the steepest part of the waves; a quartering angle lengthens the distance between peak and trough. Needless to say, quartering upwind won't help you if it leads you out to sea. It is not uncommon, however to have to resort to the paddler's version of "tacking." Getting to your objective—quiet water behind a distant point—might require several course changes to avoid taking a beam sea. For example, you might quarter upwind on a line well above your point of land and then chance surfing back into the safe haven behind the point.

Ferrying

Rather than tacking, you can employ a "ferry" as you quarter upwind into the waves. You don't need to make headway at all, but if you exert enough power to stay quartered into the wind, you will be pushed, or "ferried," sideways. That could get you to either side of a channel or to the hypothetical point of land in the previous scenario. Your ferry direction will be the direction your bow is pointed. As we will learn in a later chapter, wind is not the only force to deal with. Currents—tide-driven or in rivers—can slow or halt headway. This is also the time to use a ferry. There is an optimum combination of paddling force and the ferry angle (somewhere between zero and 45 degrees) that will cause you to move sideways, presumably toward a safe harbor.

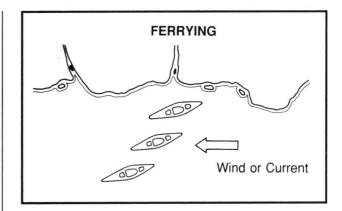

FERRYING

Wind or Current

Evasive Paddling

The right strokes will be helpful in executing evasive maneuvers. Your strokes should be flat and wide, to keep the upper blade out of the wind. Be prepared to let go with *one* hand if the wind catches a blade. If you are having trouble turning into the wind, keep your speed up and use sweep strokes. Keep trying to turn as several waves go by. Your turn may only happen at one phase of the wave and you don't want to quit too soon. Whether turning up- or downwind, remember that your boat will turn best (but be the most vulnerable) when it's sitting on top of a wave, the bow and stern out of the water.

In any troubled-water situation, your minimum strategy is to paddle forward, in some direction. Steady, forward strokes, planted solidly in the wave tops, are as good as a brace and preferable to staying put, at the mercy of the elements.

Entering and Leaving Eddies

River runners must learn early to negotiate eddies, for they are a major feature of whitewater rivers. But eddies also occur in the coastal environment, where currents resulting from tidal ex-

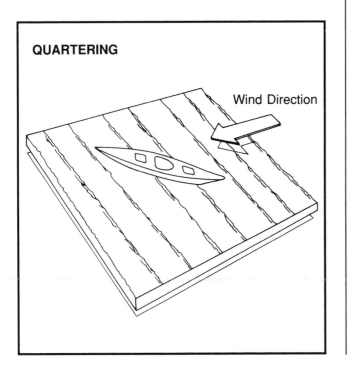

QUARTERING

Wind Direction

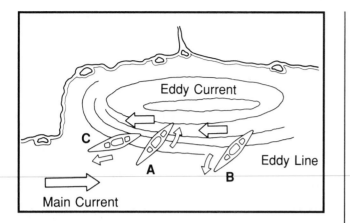

*Kayak **A**, leaving main current and entering eddy, must lean boat to left as kayak crosses eddy line. Boat **B**, leaving eddy to enter main current, must lean boat left to turn and go with current, or leave at an acute angle **C** to exit and head up current without getting turned down current.*

changes (see Chapter 7) are blocked by island and coastal features. Eddies can be both fiend and friend. An eddy is formed when moving water encounters friction, such as an opposing current, a point of land, an island, or some other obstacle. The current in the eddy (above) is going in the opposite direction of the main current. Giant eddies can form in bays or shoreline irregularities and may be used to escape the negative effects of currents that may be slowing your progress down a channel. It is not especially difficult to get into or out of such eddies; your first challenge is to recognize that such a refuge, or trap (if your eddy is going the wrong way), exists. In more confined areas, or where, say, strong currents are rushing past a rocky point, you need to know how to leave an eddy or, if you want to duck in under the point, how to enter it.

The figure above shows kayaks leaving and entering an eddy. Eddy lines can be extremely powerful, to the point where the upstream (eddy) current grabs the bow of the kayak as it enters the eddy and you are capsized downstream (relative to the main current). You must counteract the force of the eddy current by leaning your boat upstream into the turn as you drive your kayak across the eddy line. A high or low brace (described immediately below) may be needed to stabilize the kayak as you finish the eddy turn. When leaving the eddy, to head your boat downcurrent calls for leaning the kayak, also in the direction of the turn. If you wanted simply to leave the eddy and stay headed upstream—the move, if you plan to ferry across the channel—you will need to hold an acute angle upon leaving the eddy to keep from being swept downchannel. Mind you, these are fairly rare situations for most cruising, but you should learn and practice eddy turns if you are going to spend time in areas where heavy currents occur.

LEANS AND BRACES

The bracing strokes themselves are easy. What's difficult is making them reflexive. Repetitive drills and commitment to the point of capsize are the best way to get the bracing reflex into your muscle memory. Some paddlers may find that they master the Eskimo roll (described later in this chapter) before they've mastered solid braces. Forget the Eskimo roll for now; there are practice environments that will permit you to commit vigorously to the high and low brace without risking a capsize every time.

Warm, quiet water—perhaps a swimming pool—is the place to start. Your first assignment is to forget the images you may have of a paddler, arms and paddle extended above the head and stretched way out over the water. Don't confuse body lean with boat lean. Boat lean, or cocking, is the secret of a good brace. The drill is so simple as to seem unlikely.

Cocking the Boat

Sit in your kayak holding your paddle in front of you, elbows and hands low. Keeping your upper body (and paddle) immobile, use your hips—and/or lift alternate knees—to cock the boat over to one side, and then to the other. Do it slowly; do it fast. It should become a natural motion. See how much you can raise each boat edge without throwing your upper body into it. Keep your upper body perpendicular to the center line of the kayak. From time to time I'll use the term "hip snap" to describe this basic action.

The only time you should ever need to brace on your paddle is when your boat lean fails to counteract (or when it overreacts to) the effect of wave or current action on your hull. That's the kayaker's secret to navigating in sea conditions that would intimidate most powerboaters. We have the ability to make timely gyrostatic adjustments of our craft as it pitches and yaws in the ocean swells—not unlike the gimbals found on huge yachts that keep the compass and the cocktails level with the horizon. Your hips are your gyroscope.

It is worth noting here that the kayak itself is inherently seaworthy; paddlers are the problem. Put a sea kayak adrift in the center of a stormy Atlantic with a cover over the cockpit. Eventually it will wash up somewhere—right side up. No sailboat or powerboat can hope for such salvation.

Low Brace

Once you've figured out the hula hips, it's time to add the paddle. You can practice on any piece of quiet water, but if you want to commit your boat to the point of capsize, you can use the edge of a pool; a sloping beach is even better. If you start in a pool (as many kayak classes do), you don't need to be in a boat. Just sit at the pool edge, facing first one direction and then the other, and practice bracing on the pool water.

The most-used brace, which often occurs as a natural reflex, even with novices, is the low brace. The low brace uses the back, or non-power, face of the paddle blade. Sit in your boat as you did for the boat-lean drills. Your grip on the paddle shaft is the same as for a forward stroke, your wrists are cocked slightly downwards, and your elbows are higher than your wrists. Slap the back of one paddle blade, then the other, on the surface of the water. You want the blade angled so that a slap finds resistance, without the blade diving. With a feathered paddle, one blade will be in position for the low brace, but you will have to twist the wrist of your control hand upwards to get the other blade flat. Look at your blade, but it's not necessary to rotate your torso or shoulders.

So far, so good. The next step is to get your arms and paddle back into neutral and to begin cocking the boat (as described immediately above). You want to slap the back of the blade on the surface just before your boat lean puts one or the other edge under water. Try this: start by lifting your left knee while dropping the right, and just before the moment of capsize, hit the water with the back of your right blade and lift your right knee. Look squarely at your right paddle blade as you do this. Bringing your kayak flat from its right-side lean will be a result of bracing up on your right blade (your outrigger) and snapping your hips.

47

The low brace. The elbows are higher than the wrists.

Low brace with boat almost on edge.

If you find a sloping beach, you can be much more aggressive. If your paddle blade dives due to a faulty blade angle, or your timing of the hip snap is off, your paddle will hit solid matter and you can just brace up on it. In fact, you can start your drill by simply putting the non-power face of the blade on the beach, cock your boat over toward the beach, and bring the boat back to upright to get the feel of righting the kayak. Then, instead of placing the blade on the beach, slap it on the surface of the water, and keep moving away from the beach toward deeper water as you gain confidence and realize that, in fact, the water is just as firm a platform as the beach—so long as you hit it with a properly angled blade. You need to practice this on both sides until it becomes an automatic reaction.

Experienced paddlers, especially those who learned their skills on white water, often throw out braces so naturally and reflexively that you won't see it happening. Think about it: at the very moment that a kayaker completes a forward stroke and starts to recover the blade, its non-power face is angled just right, inches above the water—a brace waiting to happen!

High Brace

The only thing high about this brace is that your wrists are higher than your elbows. And there is no need to raise your elbows; they are better off low and in front of you. Too much arm and elbow extension can result in shoulder injury. The high brace uses the power face of the blade. The high brace cannot be executed as quickly as the low brace, but it is a more powerful brace and is usually reserved for dealing with a violent event. A sudden, breaking wave on a submerged reef would qualify; so would broaching (getting sideways) as you get surfed into the beach on a "dumper."

The high brace. The elbows are below the wrists.

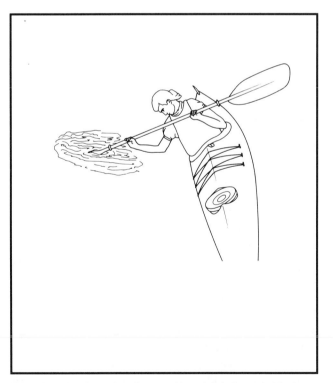

Bringing the boat back up with a high brace. Notice paddler drops head toward the blade.

Sit in your kayak near an embankment or sloping beach and set up for a brace by cocking up your forearms and wrists so that the paddle shaft is almost under your chin. Without reaching out too far, plant the power face of your paddle blade on the bank or beach. Look at your blade. See how far over you can lean your boat, even touch your nose to the water, and bring the boat back up. A major objective of this exercise is to use your paddle as a fixed point and accomplish the boat lean and recovery by snapping the hips. If you have to lift the kayak upright with main strength—arms and shoulders—you're doing a body lean rather than a boat lean. Use your knees and hips to right the kayak, not your paddle.

Once you get the feel for dropping and righting each edge of your kayak, try moving away from the beach. Now you will have to hit the water with your blade so that the water, rather than the beach, will support your lean and recovery.

Back at the shoreline, you should be able to cock the boat almost completely over until your cockpit is half submerged; then right the boat. An ultimate goal is to do the same in deep water. Lay the boat over until your face is in the water and bring it back up. Here's a tip: keep your eyes on the paddle blade and drop your chin toward the blade as you right the boat. It's that low CG thing again. Heads are heavy! Think of the brace as stopping your fall with the paddle; then pulling the kayak back under you with your knee-hip snap; your head comes up last.

If you find yourself in battlefield conditions where you need a high brace, you will not be leaning your boat over to meet water that is parallel to the horizon line. The water will be rising up to you—on your beam. You will want to cock your boat toward the wave (or breaking surf), put your paddle blade on the crest, and either ride it out or hang on until the wave passes under you.

Sweeping Brace

The high brace described above is static to the extent that your paddle blade is placed on the water at 90 degrees to your cockpit. You actually have more latitude than that. You can high-brace in an arc of almost 180 degrees, from bow to stern. The sweeping brace is not so much a stroke as it is a drill that develops a nice feel for blade orientation, boat lean, and torso rotation. It is also an above-water replication of an important component of the Eskimo roll. Sitting in your kayak (or at the edge of a pool), extend your left arm as far forward as possible, slightly opening your last three fingers. Use your control hand to make the forward blade flat or slightly "climbing" (rear edge higher than the front edge). Put the blade on the water. Your right hand should be about 6 inches from your right ear and your right elbow at your side. Now you can cock your boat to the left by lifting your right knee as you begin to sweep the blade in an arc from front to rear, keeping the blade angle climbing—lose the angle and the blade will dive, taking you with it. Your right elbow and your right hand (which is "attached" to your ear by a make-believe 6-inch string) hardly change position throughout the entire sweep. It is your torso rotating toward your stern that directs the sweeping blade. Your objective is to commit further and further to your boat lean. At any point in the sweep you should be able to lift the left knee and bring the boat back under you. As with any stroke or brace, practice it and perfect it on both sides.

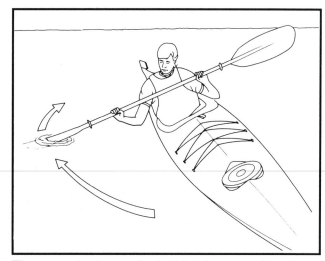

The sweeping brace. In the high brace position the paddler sweeps the blade in an arc from bow to stern.

Eskimo Roll

The debate goes something like this: a roll is a stunt, rarely called for in the paddling conditions most kayakers see, and if it is, it usually fails. Or: the roll is the single most effective self-rescue technique and a vital piece of insurance. Both statements are true, so the choice is yours.

Those of us who perfected our rolls for white-water kayaking don't face such a decision. Frankly, I've never been forced to roll a sea kayak and in my many miles of coastal cruising have never seen a paddling companion use one. Most experienced paddlers tend to subscribe to Washburne's first-line-of-defense theory and don't go looking for difficult situations. As a practical matter, most persons don't have their touring kayaks properly outfitted for performing Eskimo rolls, and the execution of a roll in a tossing sea with a fully

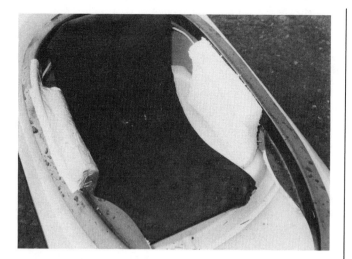

Hip clips give better control for braces and the Eskimo roll.

loaded boat is infinitely more difficult than a roll performed in the 80-degree water of a YMCA pool (the place where you most likely will learn it). All of that said, the roll is well worth learning. You will be in an elite group who put value in mastering a special skill and who can venture forth with greater confidence than their companions who have not.

Outfitting

If you turn upside down in your kayak and fall out of the seat, you can't roll. The requisites are shortened foot pegs that force your knees up into knee or thigh pads and your back against a seat back or backrest. Some padding on the sides of your seat (at the hips) will also help keep you in

a "brace-lock" position. Some of the larger cockpits of touring kayaks require ingenuity. Carved and sanded minicell foam glued in with waterproof cement is your best bet. You should seek a happy medium between a tight fit and one that interferes with long-term paddling comfort or a quick exit when required.

Learning the Roll

Go to school, join a paddling club, or get an instructor. Learning to roll without at least a confederate is beyond most people's capability. You'll have a good head start if you've already mastered the hip snap and high brace. The end point of the Eskimo roll is, in fact, indistinguishable from a high brace. Some instructional programs teach the Eskimo roll *first* so that students will not hesitate to practice aggressive bracing techniques, confident that they can roll back up if they miss.

The roll has three components: setup, sweep, and hip snap. You may hear instructors or paddlers refer to rolls with various names: "screw roll," "layback roll," "C-to-C roll," "slash roll," and so on. The setup and sweep are common to all of them, but the final component has invited a number of variations, which are usually aimed at keeping the paddler's head from coming up too soon or to make allowance for an individual's lack of flexibility. Regardless of the roll style you learn, neither muscle power nor Zen is required. There are a legion of small or average-sized women, of average athletic ability, who can roll up a kayak, using only their hands while expending about three calories of energy. The roll is 100 percent technique.

A swimming pool is the best place to learn, and a swimming face mask can help you to see what is happening. First you want to perfect your hip

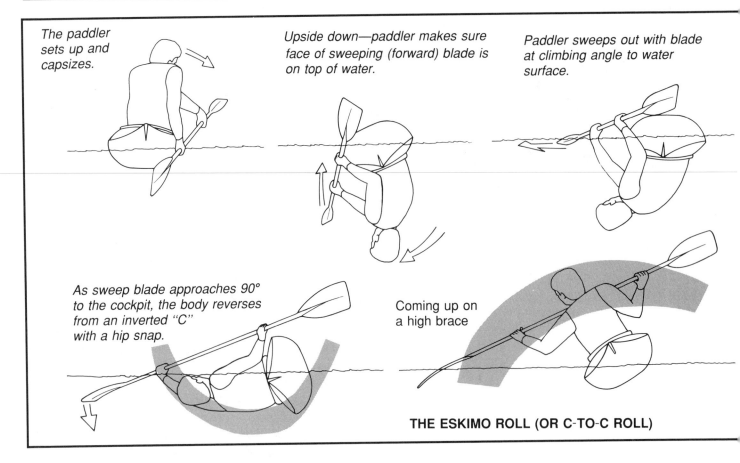

The paddler sets up and capsizes.

Upside down—paddler makes sure face of sweeping (forward) blade is on top of water.

Paddler sweeps out with blade at climbing angle to water surface.

As sweep blade approaches 90° to the cockpit, the body reverses from an inverted "C" with a hip snap.

Coming up on a high brace

THE ESKIMO ROLL (OR C-TO-C ROLL)

snap, which can be done hanging on to the edge of the pool or by holding the hands of a confederate who stands in waist-deep water at your side. Tip the boat over toward the wall (or your confederate). Without going all the way over, practice rolling, or hip-snapping, the boat back upright. There should be very little pressure on your arms. Now, go all the way over—still hanging on—and practice bringing the boat back to upright. Concentrate on cocking your boat with your hips to initiate the move. Your head should stay in the water until the kayak is almost entirely upright. Fight the urge to get your head up first; it's like trying to lift a bowling ball on the end of a pole. Once you've developed an easy boat-righting motion by hanging on to the wall, try tipping over away from the wall. Once you are upside down, reach up from the other side of the hull and grab the side of the pool (or your confederate's hands) and right the boat. This will develop your sense of orientation and test your presence of mind. If you've been doing the move correctly, at the end of a practice session your tummy muscles and knees should be sore, not your arms or shoulders.

It is possible to move directly from the pool edge to a large kickboard. Initially, have your friend hold the board while you submerge and

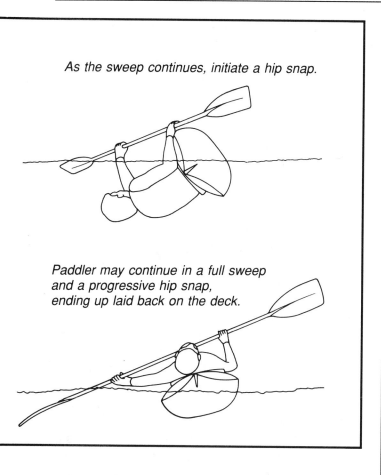

As the sweep continues, initiate a hip snap.

Paddler may continue in a full sweep and a progressive hip snap, ending up laid back on the deck.

reemerge. If you can progress to popping yourself back up without help, you are well on your way.

Set Up and Sweep

The paddle, so fundamental to our sport, also gets in our way sometimes. So now, we have to figure out what to do with that unwieldy stick to re-create the support that we found from the pool-side or kickboard.

The setup is first practiced above water. Starting out, you will capsize yourself while in the "setup" position. Under battlefield conditions, you

are usually capsized first; you have to set up underwater. To set up, put your nose on the front deck (well, get as close as your flexibility permits). If you want to come up on your right side—the usual side for a right-hand control paddler—hold your paddle with the shaft lengthwise along the left edge of the kayak, and reach well forward. Your hands should be as close to the water as you can reach. Cock the forward wrist downward so that the blade is on the same plane as the water. Visualize yourself upside down in the water in this position. When you do capsize yourself, you'll want the paddle blade surface you're looking at to end up above the water.

Capsize the boat toward your confederate while holding your position. Your friend should grab the blade and gently tap it on the surface so that you get oriented. Next the instructor should take hold of the blade and sweep it across the top of the water in a broad arc until the blade is 90 degrees from the bow. Don't fight the paddle as your instructor sweeps it. Follow the blade with your eyes and head, rotate from the torso, and keep your inside arm close to your side. Once the sweeping blade is brought to rest opposite the your cockpit, the confederate holds the blade on the surface, and you right yourself exactly as you would if you were hanging on to the side of the pool. Practice this until your helper convinces you that he is sweeping and positioning the paddle with little or no resistance from you. If you find that you are engaging in an arm-wrenching struggle, concentrate on relaxing and letting the paddle (guided by your helper) do the thinking.

When you make your first attempt to sweep the paddle without the help of a friend, your biggest challenge will be to keep the blade sweeping along the surface, not diving. As you start the sweep, think of leading the blade away from the boat with the top of your wrist. Keep the inside arm close to your body and the wrist of your sweep hand cocked so that the blade is on a climbing angle relative to the plane of water you're sweeping over. If the leading edge of the blade drops, the blade will dive, and you'll find yourself with no place to go.

Once you are able to effect a crude or muscled roll, or are successful in one out of five attempts, further refinements will generally involve tricks to keep your head underwater until the last moment. Dropping your nose toward the side of your roll at the last moment can help finish off a weak roll. Some people find that throwing their head back till it's almost lying on the back deck does the trick. The so-called layback or slash rolls succeed by keeping the head and body close to the axis of the boat (and the roll). Just as we learned in doing leans and braces, it's the boat we want to move, not our bodies.

Extended-Paddle Roll

If you need a confidence builder or a shortcut, try this: assume the setup position on the water, but rather than use the normal grip on your paddle shaft, slide the paddle forward until you can reach back with your trailing arm and grab the paddle blade; your forward hand will be in the same place relative to the deck of your kayak but will be further back on the shaft. Go through the tip-over and sweeping routines described above. The extended paddle gives you at least two advantages: the paddle blade in your hand gives you a "knob" that takes only a slight twist to ensure a climbing blade angle at the other end of the paddle, resulting in a good sweep. Most important, you will get almost twice as much leverage as usual from the paddle. The extended-paddle roll has long been a learning device for whitewater paddlers, but it is often impractical in river situations. Other than the extra second it

adds to setup time, there is no reason why the sea kayaker can't adopt this as his standard roll. The principal drawback is that you don't come up from the roll ready to paddle.

SELF-RESCUE

Paddling alone in conditions that can capsize a kayak might suggest that common sense was more important than skill. Yet if we assume that safety (and, ultimately, survival) is each person's individual responsibility, and if we recognize that even in a large group outing there may be no one near at hand to help, a self-rescue plan makes sense. That's often the case when conditions get rough. Certainly, for those highly skilled paddlers who venture forth solo, a self-rescue, the final line of defense, is essential. Swimming is usually *not* a defense in water temperatures lower than 55 degrees if the shore is more than a quarter of a mile distant.

The most universally accepted self-rescue is a paddle float rescue. We know several commercial outfitters who require that customers perform this maneuver—in the water—before allowing them to sign out a boat. You need a boat properly rigged (see page 55), a paddle, a paddle float (there are several styles), and a bilge pump.

Going through the motions on dry land or in shallow water might be all right, but as a true practice, you need to work on this in deep water. Before capsizing yourself, make sure your paddle float is in a place where you can easily get hold of it—under the deck or rear bungies, for example. Capsize yourself, making certain that you keep hold of the paddle and that after your wet exit (see earlier section) you are in a position to hold on to your kayak. The steps are as follows:

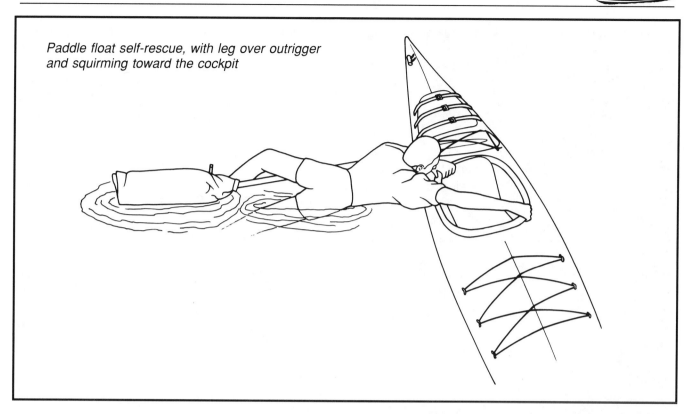

Paddle float self-rescue, with leg over outrigger and squirming toward the cockpit

1. Right the kayak (cockpit side up).
2. Squirm up on rear deck to get out of cold water.
3. Put paddle float on paddle.
4. Inflate paddle float.
5. Secure free paddle blade in rigging.
6. Reenter kayak (discussed below).
7. Reattach spray skirt.
8. Pump out your kayak.

Your reentry into the kayak relies upon the stability of the outrigger created by your paddle extended with the float. Wrap one leg around the extended paddle outrigger and get the other leg into the cockpit. You are on your stomach on the back of the kayak; squirm backwards until you can throw the leg from the outrigger into the cockpit, rotating your butt into the seat at the same time.

Keep your weight on the support of your paddle float through all of this. Once you are in the boat you can begin to empty it with the bilge pump. Try doing this *after reattaching your spray skirt,* since a real capsize is most likely to be in rough water where you may find your kayak refilling as fast as you can bail.

Another self-rescue mechanism employs inflatable sponsons. There are two advantages of the sponsons over the paddle float: first, you have support on both sides of the boat, not just the paddle float side; and second, you have a paddle to use *and* a stabilized boat once you are back

Inflatable sponsons are a more versatile self-rescue option.

in the cockpit. I carry and use the sponsons for a nonrescue purpose: for fishing from a tippy hull, the sponsons are a great stabilizer, allowing me to concentrate on my fishing. The deflated sponsons are kept under the rear deck lines with one

corner attached to the hull. To put into use, a second corner is attached (by means of male-female fastex clips), the other sponson is passed under the hull, and the other two corners are attached. The tubes require about ten puffs to inflate them—and now you have a kayak you can stand up in.

ASSISTED SELF-RESCUE

Although they are perhaps a contradiction in terms, there are a host of assisted or group rescues that have been described and taught over the years. Some are practical; some are ridiculous. Realistically, the success of any of the techniques depends largely on the skill and judgment of the rescuer(s). Whether a kayaker so skilled will be on hand when *you* "huli" in the North Atlantic is another story. But at least you should have one trick up your sleeve if a companion capsizes 30 yards ahead of you.

One simple rescue relies upon you stabilizing your comrade's kayak so that he can clamber back in. Get your kayak to the front of his boat and direct him to push down on the stern of his kayak as you lift the bow. If his kayak has a stern bulkhead behind the cockpit, this will quickly empty most of the water out, and the two of you can flip the kayak upright, bringing it alongside your own. Throw your own body over the other hull, get the victim's paddle secured somewhere, and give him a hand to help him haul himself up on his kayak, where he can work his way back into his cockpit. Such a rescue can be effected quite quickly, though it does require a certain amount of agility and presence of mind on the part of both rescuer and victim. A variation of this rescue may employ a rescue cord and the vic-

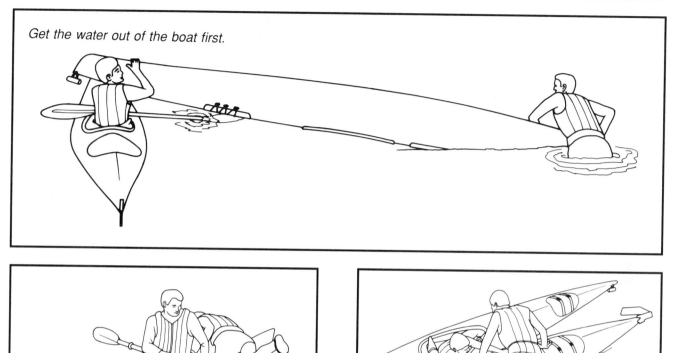

Get the water out of the boat first.

Stabilize your friend's kayak so victim can clamber in.

Paddle and stirrup rescue. Victim's paddle is under kayak to anchor stirrup rope (see diagram of hitch).

Paddle Hitch

tim's paddle to provide him a stirrup, or "leg up," as a horse person might say.

The latter rescue involves the same steps leading up to bringing the victim's emptied kayak alongside your boat. You need to have on board a heavy-duty circle of rope already sized to perform this specific rescue. Hitch one end of the rope around the middle of the victim's paddle and drop the paddle between the kayaks; turn it crossways to anchor it under your two kayaks. The other end of the rope loop is passed around each end of the victim's cockpit and leaves enough loop to droop into the water on the outboard side of the victim's kayak. He puts one foot into the stirrup and steps up into his cockpit.

These rescues, or any others you might learn

or invent, really need to be practiced in a controlled situation (such as a swimming pool), so that they can be executed quickly in a live situation. Paddlers who expect to be in a leadership position on a trip, whether by accident or design, should also be responsible for ensuring that safety and rescue gear is in their boat. These would include:

- stirrup rope (as described above)
- extra paddle float
- spare paddle
- bilge pump
- tow rope (in case a victim must be towed in his boat)
- extra clothing or means to prevent or forestall hypothermia in a victim

WIND, WAVES, AND WEATHER

If the wind never blew and you intended to paddle exclusively on small ponds and little rivers, you could simply skip this chapter—in fact you could skip the rest of this book. But even nearby lakes and impoundments are subject to wind and waves. As we will see, the waves created by motorboat traffic replicate some of the difficult situations created by nature. A few years ago, my wife and I were planning to paddle two topless kayaks up the Kona coast of the Big Island of Hawaii; it was, in fact, our first big-water kayaking adventure. Virtually all of our preparation for the trip took place on Lake Washington, a nearby lake, which is about 26 miles long and 2 miles wide. There is nothing particularly fearsome about Lake Washington; however, like most urban lakes, it is a playground for everything from jet skis to giant tugs. Add the cigarette boats, ski

boats, yachts, and dinghies, and they create a formidable "ocean."

In October we launched our surf skis at the Kona Surf Hotel. Out in the open water, we found ourselves in the towering Pacific swells. It didn't take long to adjust to the huge, but gentle, rollers. The real threat to our stability was the reflection of waves off the sheer lava walls that guard much of the Kona coast. The confusing patterns of varying height and steepness were like moguls on a moving mountain, but we quickly recognized the conditions; they were identical to the mixture of wind waves and boat wakes that often turned Lake Washington into a messy stew.

The two lessons from this are that you don't need to go to sea to encounter difficult water conditions; you can prepare for the sea in waters where the consequences of a capsize are considerably less severe. Getting dumped in 70-degree water, close to populated shores, is definitely preferable to a huli in Lake Superior or off the Maine coast.

Wind and waves are, in fact, the essence of the kayaker's environment. Their presence or absence define the experience and often the degree of risk involved in an outing, be it a day trip or month-long expedition. Like any mariner, the paddler's life is ruled by two anxieties: if the winds are calm, when will they rise?; and if they are howling, when will they drop? Read any sea kayaker's trip diary and you will understand this preoccupation.

Keep in mind, however, that the wind and waves that represent obstacles to one group of paddlers, represent a satisfying challenge to others. Just as rapids encountered on a river may be obstacles for canoe trippers, they are the essence of the sport for whitewater enthusiasts. One only needs to read the accounts of British kayakers like Frank Goodman and Derek Hutchinson, or the New Zealander John Dowd, to realize that there are folks out there who will be disappointed if they're not being buffeted and blown. Eric Soares, founding father of the Tsunami Rangers, has turned storm paddling into a sport, with special equipment and an elaborate code of operation. Hanging out on the edge, surviving a needle-threading surf landing: these are the defining elements of the sport for some.

You need not aspire to the adrenaline junkie's vision of sea kayaking, but a reasonable understanding of what's going on in the kayaker's environment—the workings of the "weather machine" (to borrow the title of Nigel Calder's book)—will not only make your outings safer ones but will greatly enhance your sense of the natural world.

And as we have already observed, the kayaker is uniquely capable of dealing with the severest conditions created by wind and waves. With a low profile, a paddler endowed with gyroscopic hips, and paddle blades that double as outriggers, the sea kayak is a creature in its element.

WIND MAKING

Anyone who has watched clouds flying across the sky in one direction and a major storm arriving from a different direction can deduce that winds and weather are related but not necessarily in a one-to-one relationship. Nevertheless, the zigs and zags of the jet stream and the global patterns that exchange warm tropical air for dry arctic air do indeed influence the local weather we experience on the ground, and the general patterns are somewhat predictable for any given locale.

You can, in fact, find historical data for rather precise areas. The chart at right is from the *Sailing Directions for the British Columbia Coast* (1973 edition) and is simply a tabulation of meteorological data, including the prevailing winds, for any given month at a very specific point along the west coast of Vancouver Island. This is useful information to have when you are embarking on a trip of a week or longer. More valuable is a small VHF weather radio dialed into the specific coastal frequencies (161.65 MHz, 162.40 MHz and 162.55 MHz are the frequencies in Puget Sound and the B.C. coast north to Alaska, for example) for your travel area.

Despite being armed with both historical data and on-the-spot updates of weather on your weather radio, you may ultimately conclude that wind and weather are ruled by chaos theory; that is, they may seem to be so inherently unstable that they are, in fact, unpredictable. The radio predicts "strong northwest winds"; instead, your

SPRING ISLAND. 50°00N 127°25W. Height above Mean Sea Level 37 feet (11m2)

MONTH	PRESSURE AT M.S.L. MEAN FOR MONTH (MB)	AIR TEMP MEAN AVERAGE (°F)	AIR TEMP MEAN DAILY MAX. (°F)	AIR TEMP MEAN DAILY MIN. (°F)	MEAN HIGHEST IN EACH MONTH (°F)	MEAN LOWEST IN EACH MONTH (°F)	EXTREME HIGHEST RECORDED (°F)	EXTREME LOWEST RECORDED (°F)	RELATIVE HUMIDITY (%)	CLOUD AMOUNT SCALE 0 TO 10	TOTAL PRECIP. AVERAGE TOTAL FALL (INS.)	TOTAL PRECIP. NO. OF DAYS	TOTAL PRECIP. MAX. FALL IN A DAY (INS.)	WIND N.	WIND N.E.	WIND E.	WIND S.E.	WIND S.	WIND S.W.	WIND W.	WIND N.W.	WIND CALM.	MEAN FORCE BEAUFORT SCALE (MPH)	NO. OF DAYS FORCE 7 AND ABOVE	NO. OF DAYS WITH FOG	NO. OF DAYS WITH THUNDER	NO. OF DAYS WITH SNOW
JANUARY	1013	40	44	37			56	13	90	7.8	12.34	23	3.04	1	28	12	35	2	6	3	6	7	4		1.1	0.4	3
FEBRUARY	1014	41	46	37			61	20	86	7.3	12.19	19	3.71	3	23	11	33	1	5	6	11	7	4		1.1	0.1	2
MARCH	1014	42	47	37			60	19	84	7.3	10.38	22	2.51	2	24	8	32	2	8	6	12	6	4		0.6	0.3	2
APRIL	1016	45	50	40			66	31	82	6.6	7.76	16	2.44	3	16	6	32	2	9	8	17	7	4		0.7	0.0	
MAY	1018	50	56	45			72	34	84	6.7	4.44	14	2.40	2	13	6	26	2	8	11	23	9	4		1.8	0.1	
JUNE	1017	54	58	49			88	40	86	7.4	4.73	14	5.87	1	7	6	30	3	9	12	22	10	4		1.6	0.2	
JULY	1019	57	62	52			94	42	86	5.3	3.24	9	1.83	2	6	6	23	2	7	13	29	12	3		4.6	0.0	
AUGUST	1018	58	63	53			89	40	88	5.8	4.03	11	3.00	1	6	9	29	2	7	10	21	15	3		6.3	0.0	
SEPTEMBER	1017	56	61	51			85	38	90	6.0	7.10	13	2.57	2	11	10	30	2	4	9	18	15	3		4.3	0.4	
OCTOBER	1015	51	55	46			71	32	89	7.1	13.28	20	4.03	1	18	10	41	1	6	5	9	8	4		2.8	1.4	*
NOVEMBER	1014	45	50	41			62	20	89	7.8	14.44	22	5.55	2	31	12	34	1	5	2	7	6	4		1.3	0.7	*
DECEMBER	1013	43	47	39			60	18	93	8.1	16.27	25	3.39	2	28	11	37	2	6	3	6	5	4		1.0	0.6	1
MEANS	1016	48	53	44						6.9				2	17	9	32	2	7	7	15	9					
TOTALS											110.11	208													27.2	4.2	8
EXTREMES							94	13					5.55														
NO. OF YEARS OBSERVATIONS																											

No. of Days column under Precipitation indicates days with fall of .01 or more inches (0.3mm.)
* Indicates less than half a day.
Authority – Data supplied by the Ministry of Transport. Air Services Meteorological Branch.

Climate data from coast piloting manual

day brings flat, calm seas. On the days when the forecaster has promised "light, variable winds," you will find yourself battling fierce headwinds. However, certain forecasts should focus your attention. If the forecaster says a storm accompanied by hurricane-force winds is centered on a point 90 miles northwest of your present location and is moving south, remain in no doubt. Make the necessary adjustments to your travel and campsite plans.

While the forecasts and tabulations always use eight points of the compass to describe wind direction, the kayaker is only conscious of four. In other words, a wind out of the southwest is simply a south wind. The effects on your environment will not change until a wind direction moves at least 90 degrees. In an area of channels, and especially in deep inlets, there are often only two wind directions: up the channel or down the channel. Thus, a west wind becomes a northwest wind in a channel that lies northwest to southeast. This is reasonable; the winds at the surface tend to conform to the valley or channel over which they blow. There is also a venturi, or compressor, effect around points, headlands, and at constrictions in an inlet or channel. Wind accelerates as it rushes past or through such obstructions. (Remember: air is a fluid, like water.)

Global winds affect large-area wind and weather patterns. Wind forecasts purport to relate to a specific area (Penobscot Bay or the Straits of Georgia, for example), but *your* winds are often related to the water and specific topography over and around which these generalized elements travel. In addition to the funneling effect of deeply incised inlets, there are numerous combinations of coastal contours and elevations that can affect, or actually create, winds.

Temperature differentials between the water body and the land mass can also create strong, localized winds. Williwaws, for example, are miniature cyclones usually associated with bodies of water lying in mountainous areas. The most common of these localized winds are convection winds, which can occur on days when the generalized weather is stable and winds aloft are light. During the day the land mass warms, and the kayaker encounters strong winds being sucked toward shore to fill the void left by rapidly rising warm air. Hence, the frequent advice to travelers in certain coastal areas to travel in the morning and get off the water before the onshore winds begin to blow. The reverse situation can result when heavier, cold air, building over the interior, can literally avalanche toward the sea, producing offshore, or katabatic, winds.

THE EFFECTS OF WIND

The kayaker has two concerns: the severity of the wave action and making headway. The ocean swell and local wind waves can collide with such features as steep beaches, rocky reefs, and tidal currents. These hazards are discussed later in the chapter, but the most common situation is one in which the force and direction of the wind make headway difficult or impossible, so that you are forced off the water well before the wave height threatens your stability. Your goal is to avoid committing yourself to a long crossing on open water where you might be put into such a position.

Every mariner should be familiar with the Beaufort scale, but you don't need to remember that large trees sway in a 30-MPH wind to protect yourself. You do need to recognize that winds rated "strong," "gale force," and above represent a "no go" for most sane paddlers. Even if a strong and technically competent paddler could

Beaufort Number or Force	Wind Speed			World Meteorological Organization Description	Estimating Wind Speed		
	Knots	mph	km/hr		Effects Observed at Sea	Effects Observed Near Land	Effects Observed on Land
0	under 1	under 1	under 1	Calm	Sea like a mirror	Calm	Calm; smoke rises vertically
1	1-3	1-3	1-5	Light Air	Ripples with appearances of scales; no foam crests	Small sailboat just has steerage way	Smoke drift indicates wind direction; vanes do not move
2	4-6	4-7	6-11	Light Breeze	Small wavelets; crests of glassy appearance, not breaking	Wind fills the sails of small boats which then travel at about 1—2 knots	Wind felt on face; leaves rustle; vanes begin to move
3	7-10	8-12	12-19	Gentle Breeze	Large wavelets; crests begin to break, scattered whitecaps	Sailboats begin to heel and travel at about 3—4 knots	Leaves, small twigs in constant motion; light flags extended
4	11-16	13-18	20-28	Moderate Breeze	Small waves 0.5—1.25 meters high, becoming longer; numerous whitecaps	Good working breeze, sailboats carry all sail with good heel	Dust, leaves, and loose paper raised up; small branches move
5	17-21	19-24	29-38	Fresh Breeze	Moderate waves of 1.25—2.5 meters taking longer form; many whitecaps; some spray	Sailboats shorten sail	Small trees in leaf begin to sway
6	22-27	25-31	39-49	Strong Breeze	Larger waves 2.5—4 meters forming; whitecaps everywhere; more spray	Sailboats have double reefed mainsails	Larger branches of trees in motion; whistling heard in wires
7	28-33	32-38	50-61	Near Gale	Sea heaps up, waves 4—6 meters; white foam from breaking waves begins to be blown in streaks	Boats remain in harbor; those at sea heave-to	Whole trees in motion; resistance felt in walking against wind
8	34-40	39-46	62-74	Gale	Moderately high (4—6 meters) waves of greater length; edges of crests begin to break into spindrift; foam is blown in well-marked streaks	All boats make for harbor, if near	Twigs and small branches broken off trees; progress generally impaired
9	41-47	47-54	75-88	Strong Gale	High waves (6 meters); sea begins to roll; dense streaks of foam; spray may reduce visibility		Slight structural damage occurs; slate blown from roofs
10	48-55	55-63	89-102	Storm	Very high waves (6—9 meters) with overhanging crests; sea takes a white appearance as foam is blown in very dense streaks; rolling is heavy and visibility is reduced		Seldom experienced on land; trees broken or uprooted; considerable structural damage occurs

The Beaufort wind scale and its effects on land and sea

deal with the waves—which will be fully white-capped in winds in the 20-MPH-and-above range—he will not be able to make any reasonable headway. Lack of progress is only part of the problem; simply hanging on to the paddle becomes a challenge when winds reach strong and gale force. Better to hole up with a pot of tea and a good book until the wind drops. An actual experience points up the wisdom of this strategy:

Our group holed up for two days on an exposed coastal section of Canada's Vancouver Island in the face of a hurricane-force storm. At noon on the third day we attempted to make a 6-mile exposed crossing, but within ten minutes determined that the effort was not worth the yield. We returned to our island, reset camp, and got out our novels. We departed at the following dawn on giant swells that the storm had produced, but the wind was dead calm and the surface of the swells was smooth. Within two hours we were safely back among the islands and protected channels that would take us home.

As we relaxed on an inside beach having our late brunch, two kayaks emerged from a channel across from us, making their weary way back to the launch site and trip end. We finished lounging on the beach and then took to the water, quickly overtaking the two kayaks. They had pressed on the previous day at the very time we were retreating to camp, and after five hours they finally made it back to the inside islands. Utterly exhausted, they were not able to get back on the water until noon the next day (when we encountered them). By attempting to fight the winds they expended tremendous energy, took unnecessary risks, and actually reached the takeout and launch site after we did. (A river or open-water trip always has a launch "put in" and landing, "take out"; in sea kayaking they are usually the same place; see Chapter 10.)

Trip plans need to allow for wind and weather delays. Striking out or remaining on the water in deteriorating conditions in order to stay on a schedule is very often the cause of sea kayaking mishaps. Leaving aside such doomsday warnings, the simple arithmetic is enough to keep you ashore when the wind picks up. Fighting a 20-MPH headwind with its attendant waves will slow a kayaker's speed down from 4 knots to 2 knots. A 10-mile day becomes a five-hour ordeal. Waiting for the wind to drop puts the destination within a morning's paddle.

Paddlers will claim that the wind only blows in their face, but despite Murphy's Law of paddling, you may have occasion to enjoy a following wind. Tail winds of 10 to 20 MPH may invite you to go surfing off toward your destination, or to put up a small sail. In winds up to 15 MPH you will be in kayaker's heaven, but if they increase, and if you are unskilled in surfing techniques, you may begin to have control problems. As the kayak is caught by following waves, it is lifted onto the crest, where it is pivoting on just a few feet of hull. If you have been relying on a rudder, the rudder, as well as the front 6 feet of kayak, may be out of water. If you survive the downhill surf, your bow will "pearl" into the back of the wave that is retreating in front of you as you slide off the crest of the wave and land broached (sideways) to the following seas. The next wave dumps on top of you. In other words, the following sea, which can give you a marvelous ride, becomes a control problem.

Even rarer than a good tail wind is a wind and wave direction that takes you precisely where you are headed. This means that at some point you will probably be forced off your "ride" and be required to take a "beam," or broaching sea (coming at your side), and this is usually the most difficult paddling condition for kayakers. You might recall the evasive strategies described in

Chapter 5, which dealt mainly with head winds. In the tail-wind scenario, you can quarter downwind until you are positioned to make the downwind ride for the last leg of your trip.

Knowing that the wind is predicted to blow at 5 to 15 MPH or that "strong" winds are forecasted is not the only thing you need to know. The effect of wind on a body of water is a function of several factors: the wind velocity, its duration and direction, the distance (or "fetch") over which the wind blows, the shape and orientation of the body of water, currents, and the depth of the water. Making headway is an obvious consideration. And if you can make headway, your ability to control the boat and stay upright may be a minimal concern during 99 percent of the passage; it's the 1 percent that involves a launch, a landing, or the rounding of an exposed point that comprise the crux of your kayak handling problems. Your trip plan must account for more than just the prevailing conditions; it must plan for these crux moves. Determining these paddling situations in advance will be your key to safe and stress-free adventures.

A simple situation might involve a launch in a protected cove, entering an open channel where a 15-MPH headwind and 2-foot waves with some whitecaps will slow your progress to less than 3 knots; you'll land 4 miles later in another protected cove on a gently sloping beach. Even paddlers of novice to intermediate skills might be willing to undertake this journey and may, in fact, enjoy the exhilaration of facing the elements. However, let's add some variations to this basic theme:

Now the next protected landing is 12 miles distant (instead of 4). Two miles down channel, you must cross a 2-mile-wide bay, and at the far side of the bay is a point jutting out into the channel. Until you reach your destination, a rocky shoreline precludes landings in anything but dead calm conditions. If you choose to set out in these conditions, you will be taking on significantly more risk, if for no other reason than time and distance. Even if wind velocity does not increase, it will have more time blowing up the channel to create higher, steeper waves. Your own energy, which might have been sufficient to sustain a speed of 3 MPH for 4 miles, is slowly sapped and at a critical point in the itinerary—approaching the far side of the bay—you could be fatigued and less capable of dealing with a difficult situation. Not only has the bay given the wind more fetch, but you've been forced away from shore. As you approach the point, you will discover that a steady 15-MPH wind translates into a 25-MPH venturi effect around the point and is accompanied by eddying currents where the wind-driven waters race past the point.

There are dozens of other variations on the above trip scenario, including wind shifts that could send you further out in the channel to avoid the clapotis (the waves reflecting off of a rocky shore), or a reversal of the tidal currents so that wind-opposing waves steepen, or simply an increase in the winds to the point where you are no longer able to make headway. A deep channel that is intersected by a tributary river might result in a bar deposited by the river. In this case, the evenly spaced 2-foot waves that you so easily navigated in deep water are exploding on the river bar. Wave energy that was proceeding uninterrupted up the deep channel is now released vertically. You'll either have to go far out in the channel to get around the bar, or else attack the breakers head on, prepared to brace as you plunge through the confusion. The map on pages 66 and 67 shows a hypothetical body of water and a host of land-water characteristics that can produce more excitement at the margin than a trip planner has bargained for.

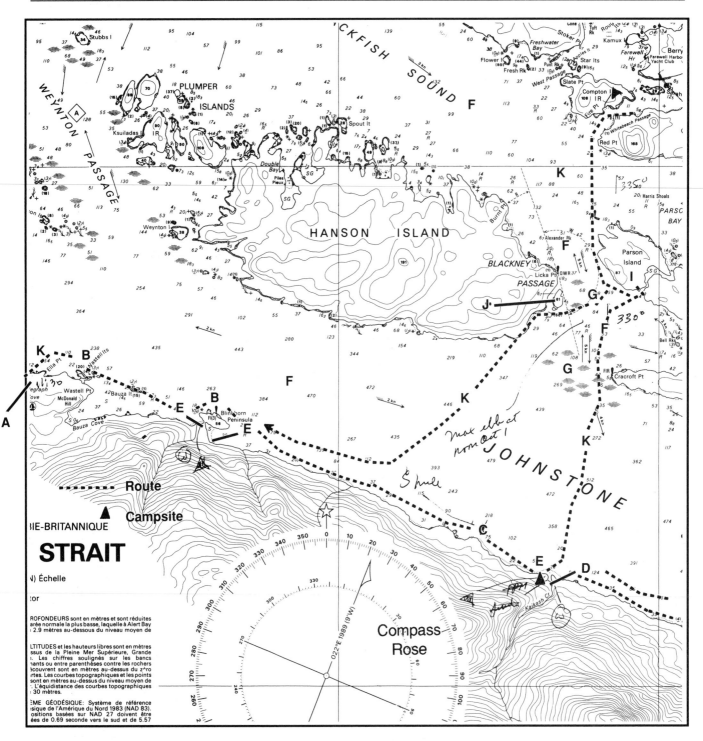

Route

▲ Campsite

STRAIT

Compass
Rose

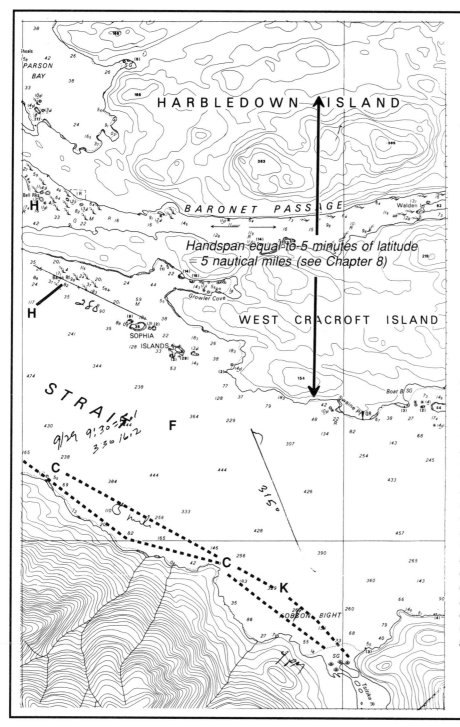

Handspan equal to 5 minutes of latitude = 5 nautical miles (see Chapter 8)

(**A**) An extremely protected launch. Know what awaits you out in the channel. (**B**) Prominent points create an acceleration of wind and currents around them; even less prominent ones, like (**C**), have significant effect. (**D**) An incoming river creates a gravel bar where wave action can become exaggerated. (**E**) Look for bays with sand or gravel beaches indicated; may be a good place to hide or get to in a blow. May be the only place to land and camp. (**F**) A long strait funnelling winds and currents to and from the ocean can cause problems. Note the current speed and direction symbols. The arrow with the tail is flood and without is ebb. The narrow constriction at Blackney Passage causes the currents to accelerate. (**G**) Strong currents, narrow passages, and points of land are ingredients for tide rips. (**H**) Kelp beds can help you and hinder you, depending on conditions and location. (**I**) Narrow passages like this can be a shortcut only if the tide is up and the current slack. With the ebbing tide it becomes a river filled with rapids. (**J**) This narrow passage becomes an exciting place when the currents are at maximum flood or ebb. (**K**) The dashed line shows an actual route. Any points of land and the channel itself present a challenge in wind and current, but **K** signifies the "Crux" moves: the first exposure to open water after launch, crossing an open bay like Robson Bight, a direct crossing of the strait (fog, wind, current, and ship traffic pose hazards), and anywhere the waterway opens up toward open ocean. (See Chapter 8 for more discussion of seamanship.)

WAVE MAKING

Waves are essentially a product of the wind, but they are also created by tidal currents, which are similar to river currents. These so-called standing waves are stationary (whether as a result of tide-driven currents or river gradient), whereas wind-driven waves are moving over the water (and the water content is the same in any one wave). There is an entire science of wave formation, and it's largely a mathematical discipline that factors in the time and distance over which the wind blows on a body of water along with the steepness of the beach (or other obstacle lying in the water's path) to calculate the breaking point of the wave. Roughly speaking, a wave breaks when its height reaches one-seventh of its length (measured from crest to crest).

The most common breaking waves are the surf on beaches. The steeper the beach, the more quickly wave energy is forced upward to create a "dumping" surf. Chapter 9 discusses strategies for dealing with surf, which can occur even when wind and swell are minimal. Breaking waves beyond the surf zone are the result of high winds, and it is their steepness and their tendency to break, not their height, that threatens the paddler's stability. Ocean swell, discussed in the section just below, can attain enormous heights (measured from trough to crest) and still be easily negotiable by a kayaker. And wind waves of up to 3 feet in height can be handled by intermediate paddlers until headway (due to winds) becomes a problem. As waves increase beyond this point, you may eventually have to deal with an obstacle or a landing, and it is here that their height becomes a matter of real concern. Knowing that a landing on a windward (that is, relative to your kayak), or protected, beach is near at hand will reduce your anxiety considerably.

You already know that physical obstacles—beaches, reefs, rocks—will cause waves to steepen and break. But waves can also collide with opposing water currents, and the result can be much like waves hitting a beach. The waves get steep as the distance from crest to crest gets compressed, and they may begin to break, becoming actual overfalls in extreme situations. Conversely, current and wind running in a same direction may lengthen and attenuate the waves —a paddler's dream, if you happen to be going their way.

Which brings us back to those waves that are not wind-related at all but, like a river, are associated with the movement of currents and gradient. The currents and gradient are the result of tidal exchange, as ebbing waters leave a bay, sound, inlet, or other shorebound feature and then return (in the flood tide). Many factors influence timing of tidal currents and their speed, but you will not need a Ph.D. in wave making to appreciate that waters entering and leaving a long, narrow inlet will be moving fast if there is a twelve foot difference between high and low tide. We'll talk about tides and currents in the following chapter, but with respect to their wave-making potential, they can rival the wildest whitewater river runs. Tidal falls, whirlpools, 2-foot eddy lines, and surfing waves like those that occur regularly at British Columbia's Skookumchuck Narrows (located between Vancouver Island and the mainland) can make a Class IV river look tame.

The most commonly encountered waves resulting from tidal currents are called "tide rips." Their locations are quite predictable and many charts will indicate the venues of particularly vigorous ones, or ones in areas with high boating traffic. The term *tide rip* tends to be used generically to describe a range of disturbances, from easily negotiated standing waves, to technically demanding eddy lines, to wildly intimidating overfalls. To a novice who doesn't understand the cause of this commotion arising in his otherwise placid journey, even the standing waves can be utterly unnerving. Unfortunately, there may be enough turbulence associated with a particular tide rip that the flustered paddler responds inappropriately and capsizes himself. Usually, a few vigorous forward strokes, maybe a low brace, and a quick adjustment to boat direction relegates a tide rip to the category of mild adventure.

SWELL

A paddler venturing into coastal waters unguarded by barrier islands, reefs, or man-made jetties and the like, will encounter swell. Swell is the residual of storm waves from a disturbance long since dissipated and possibly hundreds or even thousands of miles distant. It is not uncommon to tune in the coastal weather and hear reports of 15-foot swells. That sounds awesome, but if local winds are light or calm, the kayaker may be in for an incredible thrill. There are few sensations more invigorating than riding over the crests and down the troughs of giant swells. It's as close to human flight as you can get. The dangers are more apparent than real, but there is a period of time while you are in the trough that you may lose track of impending obstacles—like a reef or barely submerged rocks. When the swell encounters such obstacles, where will the water go? Usually, straight up, and that accounts for the spectacular breaking waves that sometimes seem to arise on an otherwise calm sea. Needless to say, when you're poised on the crest of a giant swell, that's the time to assess the water conditions on your intended course.

FOG

One of the perverse challenges of the coastal environment is that the most common fog—radiation fog—is almost always in the absence of wind, or in winds under 3 MPH. Sea kayakers commonly discover that the admonition to get on the water early and avoid the wind means setting out in dense fog. Depending upon your intended route and your navigational skills (we'll get into navigation tricks in the next chapter), that's usually preferable, since the pattern for radiation fog is a gradual burning off within three to four hours of sunrise. Here is one of the paddler's most uplifting sensations: the emergence of headlands, beaches, or sunlit mountains as you approach your destination, having followed with unquestioning faith the course dictated by your compass. Combine huge ocean swell, windless seas, and a thick fog and you have a physical and sensory experience that will test your faith to the utmost. Later such experiences are recounted to your incredulous landlubber friends as "no big deal."

Radiation fog is common when clear, sunny days are followed by much colder nights, as it forms over land and later descends into the valleys and spills out over the water. We'll call it a "good" fog, because it shouldn't be confused with its more dangerous cousin, sea fog.

Caused by the interaction of moist, warm air with cold coastal waters, sea fogs are often accompanied by strong winds and may encompass huge areas. They can last for days. Paddlers have been known to set off on a warm sunny morning, dressed for the beach, only to find themselves caught by a wind-driven sea fog that can chill an unprepared paddler right to the bone. Unlike radiation fog, sea fog does not burn off—or at least, not very quickly. As it flows in and encounters a warmer land mass, this may simply create onshore winds that bring in still more sea fog. Needless to say, navigating in thick fog with a stiff wind from any quarter is not where you want to be, so pay attention to the marine forecasts concerning sea fogs and be alert to those offshore fog banks that may soon move in to engulf you. Don't assume they are going to burn off or dissipate like your common radiation fog.

TIDES, CURRENTS, BEACHES, AND BAYS

The previous chapter was an intimidating recitation of the many actual and potential hazards to carefree cruising. The next section on beaches holds out some hope of salvation, but not without it's own share of warnings: of steep beaches, boulder-blocked beaches, and, worse, no beaches. Mountain climbers are fond of making a distinction between "subjective" and "objective" risks: the former are storms, avalanches, loose rock, and the sorts of catastrophes seen as acts of God; objective factors are altitude, vertical distance, the pitch of walls and slopes—that is, measurable qualities. Chapter 6 dealt with subjective elements. No matter how carefully the sea kayaker monitors weather forecasts, or how well he or she reads the atmospherics, bad weather, strong winds, and dense fogs can move in quickly and unexpectedly. The subject of this chapter— beaches and bays, tides and currents—are ob-jective factors; you can find them on a map or read them out of a table.

BEACHES

Beaches might well have been included in the previous chapter because they are, to a great extent, the creature of wind and waves. At the same time, certain beaches can be your refuge when wind and waves create troubled waters. In contrast to the weather, which is inherently unpredictable, beaches are a comparatively objective element in the kayaker's environment.

Good charts are the place to start, as they hold many clues to the location and characteristics of beaches. Chart reading is covered in the next chapter, so, for the moment, we'll suggest an even better way. If you travel with someone who knows the area, he or she will already have scoped out the best beaches for an entire range of wind directions, swell patterns, tide levels, and even the seasons of the year. The next best option is to have a paddler who is familiar with an area mark your chart. Knowing the location of a tiny pocket beach on the windward shore—that's the quiet side—of an island when you get caught in a blow could be a lifesaver. Let's consider the attributes of beaches that can help you or hurt you.

From a kayaker's perspective, the perfect beach for sunbathing and volleyball will not be the best refuge in a blow. Beach camping is a popular objective for touring kayakers, but you may have to sneak up on the corners of that beautiful crescent of sand to keep from getting pummeled. Not surprisingly, the conditions that create finely pulverized sand—shallow and exposed coastal bays—are the least inviting to a sea kayaker in search of a safe harbor. The broad, gradually sloping beach so dear to the heart of beachcombers is the mother of spilling surf, as wave energy piles up in the shallow water. If you wish to land without surfing, you will probably have to go in at the extreme ends, the horns of the crescent, where rocky protuberances may break up the incoming swells and conceal a section of beach offset from the predominant direction of the swell (see Chapter 9 for surf landing techniques).

The other extreme is a shoreline so rockbound, steep, or impenetrable that your challenge is to find a beach at all. Even the slightest swell or wave action renders such shorelines useless, and here is where a good guide, local knowledge, or a well-marked map will be invaluable. Deep indentations—unless they receive the swell directly, thus amplifying the surf—are the classic refuge of the sea kayaker. These little bays are often too small to provide comfort to the yachtsman, but here the kayaker can slip in—and out of harm's way.

Wherever you find your beach, there will be many factors to consider. The first characteristic is simply protection; that is, the more protected the beach, the less concern you will have about the other critical beach elements (composition and steepness). A boulder-strewn or rocky beach in a deeply indented bay might be a welcome landfall compared to a sandy incline exposed to swells and the open sea. Charts will indicate the nature of the beach composition ranging from mud, sand, pea gravel, or cobble, to boulders, and sometimes a combination. The combinations are more likely to be from foreshore to shore, rather than laterally along the beach. This is where an examination of the steepness of the beach and the size of the tides will be an important consideration in your trip plan. You may have beaches that are rocky and heavily cobbled at low tide, sandy at mid-tide, and log-infested at high tide. The season of the year may be a factor as well. Sand and gravel beaches will become more steep over the course of the winter as storms push up berms. Early spring may surprise the kayaker as he collides abruptly with the same beach that he was able to charge and ascend in late summer.

As we move to the subject of tides, consider this: beaches will tend to be steeper the higher up the beach you are, and, therefore, in the flatter, low-tide region of the beach you will find friendlier "spilling" surf (at low tide). The more dynamic and intimidating "dumping" surf may greet you at high tide as the waves collide with the steep part of the beach.

At low tide, this gently sloping beach looks innocuous.

These exposed boulders at low tide present little problem; there's plenty of sand.

These logs are above the high tide line—most of the time. For now, they are a windbreak, kayak moorage, and furniture.

TIDES

Tides are a grand subject, and you can easily learn more than you need to know, like about the phases of the moon and the global displacement of seas. But you'll be better served by simply knowing *why* they're important and learning to relate chart symbols and data to the tide tables.

Tides are minimal near the equator and in the Arctic, but as we move up or down in the latitudes we discover tide differentials (between high and low) of 10 to 20 feet. Deep bays or channels can amplify the range of high and low water to 40 feet in some areas. The following is a list of things to pay close attention to when the difference between high and low tides is 6 feet or more:

Visual Appearance

Unlike rivers and lakes, whose familiar shorelines are easy to remember, the ocean shoreline you left at dawn, at low tide, may look unfamiliar when you return in mid-afternoon, at high tide. Know your compass positions and use land contours to pinpoint your location and/or destination.

Launching and Landing

You may find yourself landing within 50 feet of your campsite in the evening and arising early the next morning for a half-mile hike to a launch. The sandy incline you slid into at landing, transforms into a slimy, seaweed covered cobble at morning's launch.

Route

The inside passage you had planned in order to avoid the wind is now too shallow. Waves are steeper and more pronounced in the shallow water; worse, your direct line across the bay is now a tidal flat with only 2 inches of water. Get out and wade and drag your kayak to a deeper channel (we've all done it). Here's more bad news: shallow water is slow water. You'll expend 30 percent more energy paddling a boat in 1 foot of water than in water that's 10 feet deep.

Sea State

As we've already discussed in the previous chapter, the change of the tides can often produce strong currents, eddy lines, and standing waves (rips), and if those currents are going opposite the wind direction, they can create steep waves— even breaking waves.

Get Above High Tide

It's a good idea to make a mental note when you pull up on the beach at lunchtime—or any time— as to whether the tide is coming in or going out. You may decide to take a little hike around the island and return fifteen minutes later to find your kayak has gone to sea by itself. Pull it well up; tie it. Setting your campsite on the beach requires that you are above where the high tide line will be. Don't let those giant bleached logs fool you. Many a kayaker has camped amongst the logs to discover at 3:00 A.M. that both his tent and the logs are awash.

TIDE TABLES

The time and height of tides published in your local newspaper or in the little booklets carried in bait-and-tackle stores are obviously for the specific locale served. All such tables are based on predictions published by the National Oceanic and Atmospheric Administration (NOAA). In the more comprehensive tables available through nautical supply stores, or from paddlesports retailers in coastal areas, tide tables and current tables are combined in one book for a coastal region. Major reference points are coastal or port cities, and subsidiary tables of correction factors for a host of less prominent points (designated "secondary ports") are included; for these you must add to or subtract from the time and height predictions of the reference point. Further complicating the calculations, most tide tables are presented in standard time, requiring the addition of one hour for daylight saving time. There's a wealth of other information in the tide tables, including detailed (if not always clear) instructions on how to use them. The figures on pages 75–77 show a sample tide table (below), a secondary port (page 76), and the format for figuring the tides for the secondary port (page 77). For a trip of several days or longer, take the time to construct—you can use a computer spreadsheet—your own tide table with all adjustments made. Jot on your chart a prediction of high and low tides, for your first day; for example: "9:15 A.M., + 12; 3:30 P.M., + 2." (You may only need to be concerned about the tide heights during daylight hours.) By adding fifty minutes for each successive day, you will be close enough for most of your purposes.

I've taken lots of day trips, paying little attention to the tide tables. Let's face it; we plan our days around available time, favorable weather, our eating habits (breakfast at 7:30), and even our bowels and biorhythms. If you are unwilling to adjust your itinerary to the tides, you just have to be willing to adjust your execution to the inconveniences that tidal actions may create. That's no excuse for not knowing how to read a tide table. But suppose you lost yours, or couldn't locate one, or are just too cheap to buy one. By sight and smell you can often tell, when you arrive at water's edge, whether you are at high, middle, or low tide, and after several hours

Tide tables for Victoria, a primary port

	July								August						
	Time	Height			Time	Height			Time	Height			Time	Height	
	h m	ft	cm		h m	ft	cm		h m	ft	cm		h m	ft	cm
1 W	0050	9.5	290	**16** Th	0140	8.2	250	**1** Sa	0335	8.0	244	**16** Su	0345	7.1	216
	0935	-0.1	-3		1000	1.7	52		1035	2.2	67		1025	3.9	1.19
	1910	8.0	244		1915	7.7	235		1720	8.3	253		1710	7.8	238
	2120	7.7	235		2215	7.2	219		2315	5.0	152		2315	5.0	152
2 Th	0155	9.1	277	**17** F	0230	7.8	238	**2** Su	0440	7.2	219	**17** M	0440	6.7	204
	1015	0.2	6		1035	2.2	67		1110	3.3	101		1050	4.5	137
	1920	8.0	244		1840	7.7	235		1750	8.5	259		1730	7.9	241
	2230	7.2	219		2305	6.7	204								
3 F	0303	8.5	259	**18** Sa	0320	7.3	223	**3** M	0020	4.3	131	**18** Tu	0000	4.5	137
	1100	0.9	27		1100	2.7	82		0555	6.4	195		0540	6.3	192
	1840	8.1	247		1835	7.8	238		1150	4.4	134		1115	5.2	158
	2335	6.5	198						1825	8.7	265		1750	8.0	244

A D D O N E H O U R F O R D A Y L I G H T S A V I N G T I M

				MINUTES		HEIGHT					
									.0	4.9	4.9
									8.2	4.9	
								,.0	8.2	4.9	
							..	5.2	8.4	5.1	
							J.97	5.2	8.5	5.1	
					J 51	+0.1	0.0	5.2	8.6	5.2	
					+1 11	*1.01	*1.01	5.2	8.6	5.2	
				+0 27	+1 04	*0.96	*0.96	4.9	8.1	4.9	
	....nd. ...	48 34	122 53	+0 26	+0 44	*0.93	*0.93	4.6	7.8	4.8	
	....nd........	48 36	122 57	+0 33	+0 56	*0.90	*0.90	4.5	7.6	4.7	
	annel										
	...c irdson, Lopez Island...........	48 27	122 54	-0 21	-0 11	*0.87	*0.87	4.2	7.3	4.5	
	Friday Harbor, San Juan Island......	48 33	123 00	+0 35	+0 56	*0.92	*0.92	4.5	7.7	4.8	
	Strait of Georgia										
1135	Echo Bay, Sucia Islands.............	48 45	122 54	+1 01	+1 34	+0.1	0.0	5.2	8.6	5.2	
1137	Ferndale.....................	48 50	122 43	+0 49	+1 20	+0.5	0.0	5.6	9.0	5.4	
1139	Blaine, Semiahmoo Bay..............	49 00	122 46	+0 59	+1 27	+0.9	+0.1	5.9	9.5	5.6	
	Haro Strait										
1141	Kanaka Bay, San Juan Island.........	48 29	123 05	-0 11	-0 02	*0.86	*0.86	4.2	7.3	4.5	
1143	Roche Harbor, San Juan Island.......	48 37	123 09	+0 29	+0 52	*0.90	*0.90	4.4	7.5	4.7	
1145	Turn Point, Stuart Island..........	48 41	123 14	+0 24	+0 47	*0.90	*0.90	4.4	7.5	4.7	
	Boundary Pass										
1147	Patos Island Wharf.................	48 47	122 58	+1 03	+1 30	+0.2	0.0	5.3	8.6	5.2	
	BRITISH COLUMBIA					on VICTORIA, p.63						
	Passages inside Vancouver Island <3>										
1149	Sooke, Vancouver Island................	48 22	123 44	-0 11	-0 33	+0.8	+0.5	- -	6.4	6.6	
1151	Esquimalt, Vancouver Island............	48 26	123 26					- -	6.2	6.3	
1153	VICTORIA, Vancouver Island.............	48 26	123 23		Daily predictions			- -	6.1	6.3	
					on VANCOUVER, p.67						
1155	Sidney, Haro Strait....................	48 39	123 24	-1 01	-1 12	*0.71	*0.61	- -	7.8	7.1	
1157	Fulford Harbor, Saltspring Island......	48 46	123 27	-0 55	-1 08	-3.5	-1.0	- -	8.0	7.6	
1159	Active Pass, Mayne Island..........	48 52	123 20	-0 16	-0 30	'. 5	-0.8	- -	9.8	8.6	
1161	Cowichan Bay............... >...	48 45		-0 52				- -	8.0	8.1	
1163	Chemainus, Stuart Channe'								8.0	8.3	
1165	Ladysmith......								9		
1167	Sand Hea--										
1169	»»'.										

Correction factors for the Sooke area, a secondary port closer to your intended destination. Victoria tides and times must be adjusted accordingly.

on the water, it usually becomes apparent. From the moment at which you identify either high or low tide, you have about six hours and fifteen minutes until the next turn. That's a convenient bit of knowledge, as it also tells tide ta-ble–less travelers that for each succeeding day, the time of the high or low tide advances almost an hour (actually, about fifty minutes, as we noted above).

Yes, the tides are largely controlled by the gravitational pull of the moon and, to a lesser extent, the sun. Consequently, depending upon the phase of the moon, and it's periodic alignment with the sun, which will create extreme tides, tide differences between high and low can vary considerably. Being aware of the tidal norms, as well

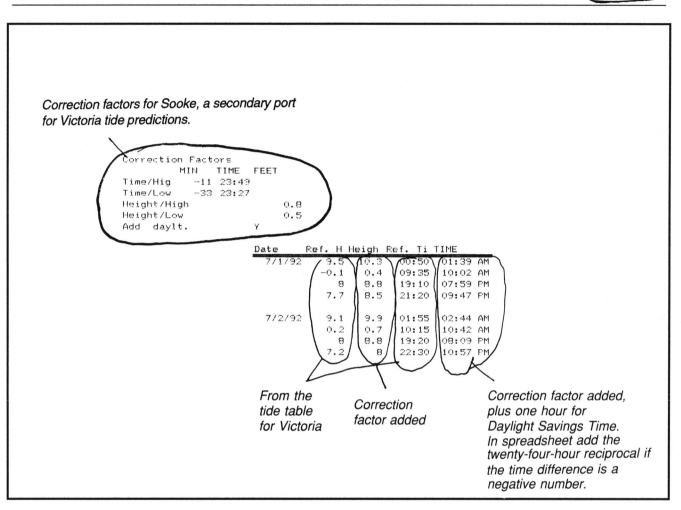

Correction factors for Sooke, a secondary port for Victoria tide predictions.

```
Correction Factors
              MIN   TIME   FEET
Time/Hig     -11  23:49
Time/Low     -33  23:27
Height/High                0.8
Height/Low                 0.5
Add   daylt.            Y
```

```
Date      Ref. H Heigh Ref. Ti TIME
7/1/92      9.5   10.3  00:50  01:39 AM
           -0.1    0.4  09:35  10:02 AM
            8      8.8  19:10  07:59 PM
            7.7    8.5  21:20  09:47 PM

7/2/92      9.1    9.9  01:55  02:44 AM
            0.2    0.7  10:15  10:42 AM
            8      8.8  19:20  08:09 PM
            7.2    8    22:30  10:57 PM
```

From the tide table for Victoria

Correction factor added

Correction factor added, plus one hour for Daylight Savings Time. In spreadsheet add the twenty-four-hour reciprocal if the time difference is a negative number.

as the extremes, should be part of your trip planning, but they need not always represent a problem. Extreme low tides (represented in the tables by negative numbers, with minus signs) are a delight to beachcombers, clam diggers, and anyone who wants a peek at underwater mysteries that are only periodically revealed. Extreme high tides, on the other hand, may permit navigation of hidden channels, the ascent of a river estuary, or the exploration of shallow bays that are mud flats under normal conditions.

A spread sheet—useful for longer trips. Once the data is entered, hide the reference port data columns, only leaving a date, height, and time.

CURRENT TABLES

Tides are the vertical movement of water; currents are the horizontal movement. Current tables look somewhat like tide tables (they are often contained in the same book), and like tide tables, there are primary reference points—a buoy in the middle of Rosario Strait, for example—and correction tables (for time and speed) for subsidiary points. Each current table indicates the direction, in compass degrees, of the ebb (going out) and the flood (coming in). See the example of a current table (below). Tides and currents are close relatives, but trying to predict the timing and strength of currents solely on the basis of high and low tides is difficult. Sometimes, however, they are your only guide. The nature of the relationship is not self-evident because of the number and complexity of factors at play. These include the size of the tide, the shape of an embayment, the inlet or coastal profile, and, especially, the size and complexity of a basin. A very large basin like Puget Sound, filled with islands and spawning its own satellite system of bays, inlets, and estuaries, is more like a river relative to the oceanic waters that regularly flood into, and ebb out of, its deep basins. All of these factors enter into the nature of the tidal exchange and govern the strength and direction of currents, making their prediction a chancy art. Furthermore, the precise location of the current measurement is often unstable, or it may be irrelevant to the normal routes

---

Current table for Admiralty Inlet showing times of slack and maximum currents and compass direction of flood and ebb currents.

Admiralty Inlet (off Bush Pt.), Washington, 1992

CURRENTS

F—Flood, Dir. 180° True   E—Ebb, Dir. 005° True

	October				October				November				November				December				December		
	Slack	Maximum			Slack	Maximum			Slack	Maximum			Slack	Maximum			Slack	Maximum			Slack	Maximum	
	h m	h m	knots		h m	h m	knots		h m	h m	knots		h m	h m	knots		h m	h m	knots		h m	h m	knots
1 Th	0249 0917 1553 1919	0552 1217 1738 2351	2.4F 1.8E 0.6F 3.0E	**16** F	0205 0842 1526 1814	0513 1139 1652 2301	2.3F 1.7E 0.4F 3.0E	**1** Su	0355 1032	0006 0707 1357 1926	2.4E 1.9F 1.8E •	**16** M	0321 1000 1739 2024	0638 1323 1901	2.4F 2.3E 0.3F	**1** Tu	0354 1016	0022 0705 1359 1958	1.9E 1.7F 2.2E •	**16** W ◑	0353 1002 1754 2228	0037 0700 1345 2006	2.3E 2.2F 3.0E 1.1F
2 F	0345 1017 1720 1954	0651 1322 1838	2.1F 1.6E 0.3F	**17** Sa	0253 0936	0606 1241 1750 2354	2.2F 1.6E • 2.8E	**2** M ◑	0453 1117	0109 0804 1458 2043	2.0E 1.7F 1.9E •	**17** Tu ◑	0420 1046 1835 2211	0049 0736 1420 2023	2.4E 2.2F 2.5E 0.6F	**2** W	0447 1050 1927 2258	0126 0753 1449 2112	1.6E 1.5F 2.4E 0.4F	**17** Th	0457 1042 1850	0146 0755 1441 2123	1.8E 1.8F 3.3E 1.4F
3 Sa ◑	0446 1119	0046 0755 1436 1952	2.6E 1.8F 1.5E •	**18** Su ◐	0349 1032	0702 1344 1901	2.1F 1.7F •	**3** Tu	0554 1159 2020 2333	0218 0858 1548 2156	1.7E 1.5F 2.2E 0.4F	**18** W	0526 1130 1924	0205 0831 1518 2140	2.1E 1.9F 2.9E 1.1F	**3** Th	0548 1123 1959	0235 0840 1534 2215	1.3E 1.2F 2.5E 0.8F	**18** F	0610 1123 1942	0310 0854 1538 2231	1.5E 1.4F 3.5E 1.9F

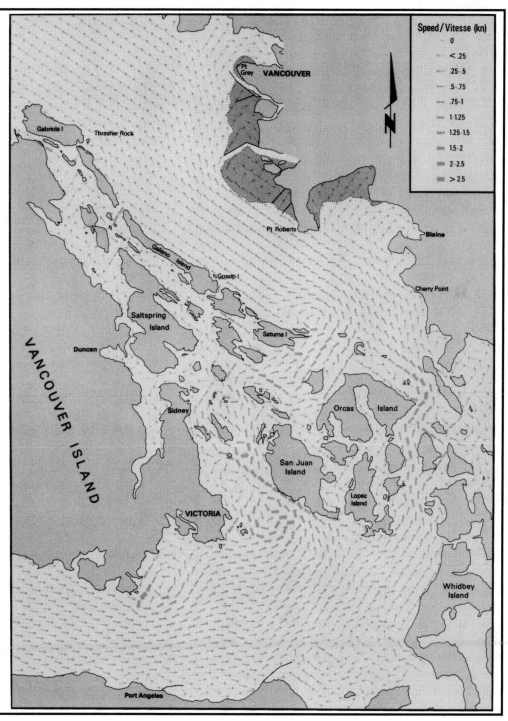

From the Current Atlas *published by the Canadian Hydrographic Service for the Puget Sound area. There are almost one hundred charts, requiring supplementary tables to match up current patterns with specific days and hours.*

traveled by kayaks. For example, a current measured and predicted for mid-channel may result in an eddy whose direction and force are completely the opposite for the shore-hugging kayaker.

Despite the highly complicated nature of currents and the unreliability of predictions, paddlers in areas where tidal differences exceed several feet, and where the waterways are heavily channeled, incised, or otherwise constricted, need to plan accordingly. Fortunately, some areas are extremely well documented (Puget Sound being one of them), and for very hazardous areas, like narrow constrictions and channels connecting two larger bodies of water, the maximum current, its speed and direction, are often indicated right on the nautical chart.

Current direction and speed can have a significant effect on a kayaker. It's simple arithmetic: 3 knots of cruising speed minus a 1 knot opposing current yields 2 knots of actual cruising speed; *add* 1 knot to your cruising speed if it's going your way. Currents of less than 1 knot will not be particularly troublesome, but at 1 knot and greater, strategies and course execution may have to be altered. Where currents begin to approach and exceed normal paddling speeds (3 to 4 knots), you can find yourself, in the worst situation, going backwards. It can be equally frustrating to overshoot a coastal destination because your dead reckoning was based on an average speed of 3 knots and your actual, current-assisted speed over the water turned out to be 5 knots. The availability of accurate current predictions can make the planning and execution of certain trips highly gratifying: for example, making a 20-mile circumnavigation of an island in four hours by riding a flood north, having lunch, waiting for the currents to reverse, and catching the ebb south. Planning can also protect you from dangerous situations, such as finding yourself in a channel where southerly winds and waves collide with a southward ebbing current. Channel crossings where currents from either direction exceed 2 knots require course planning (discussed in the following chapter) and ferrying techniques to compensate.

A plan that takes into account and either avoids or utilizes currents is, of course, ideal. Often, the reality, especially on a multiday trip, is that the plan gets preempted by events, or is impractical. Impromptu route changes, extra layover days, and schedules more in tune with waking and eating habits often take precedence over the mind-numbing study of densely packed tables and the myriad calculations and adjustments such a plan seems to require. Sometimes your careful calculations just turn out to be wrong!

Making adjustments on the fly is not such a bad thing, in any event. Sometimes a pair of binoculars trained on an area of tidal rips (or other current-induced disturbances) is better than a table-based calculation. Set to cross an exposed channel to a point ominously named Boiling Reef in the Canadian Gulf Islands, we poured ourselves another cup of coffee, wrote in our diaries, and simply waited for an hour and a half to set out. When our visual inspection satisfied us that the tidal rips were vanishing with the slackening currents, we started across.

You won't need a table to tell you when you're in an opposing current, especially if you've got a reference point like a buoy or point of land; it feels as if you're paddling up a hill of molasses. If you don't want to fight the current, it is often possible to get in tight to the shoreline. Here, currents are attenuated by friction, and you'll find back eddies that actually propel you in your direction of travel—opposite the direction of the current. (See

Washburne's tables; Chart 37 represents the currents at 5 P.M. on 9/8/92.

September 1992 currents

Tidal Range	Flood	Ebb
Large	Charts 1–8	Charts 22–29
Medium	Charts 9–15	Charts 30–36
Small	Charts 16–21	Charts 37–42
0 means negligible current at that time.		

TOP LINE: DATE, FOLLOWED BY TIME OF DAY
2ND LINE: DAY OF WEEK, FOLLOWED BY CHART FOR EACH HOUR ABOVE

Corrected for Daylight Saving Time

Date	Day	1	2	3	4	5	6	7	8	9	10	11	12	13	14	15	16	17	18	19	20	21	22	23	24
1	TU	27	28	1	2	3	4	5	6	7	37	38	39	40	41	9	10	11	12	13	14	22	23	24	25
2	WE	26	27	28	1	2	3	4	5	6	7	37	38	39	40	41	9	10	11	12	13	14	22	23	24
3	TH	25	26	27	28	1	2	3	4	4	5	6	7	8	38	40	41	16	17	18	19	20	22	23	24
4	FR	25	25	26	27	28	29	2	3	4	4	5	6	7	8	38	39	40	41	16	17	19	20	22	23
5	SA	24	25	25	26	27	28	29	2	3	4	4	5	6	7	8	38	38	39	40	41	42	18	20	30
6	SU	31	31	32	33	33	34	35	36	2	3	4	4	5	6	7	8	38	38	39	40	41	42	17	19
7	MO	20	30	31	32	32	33	34	35	36	2	3	4	4	5	6		8	38	38	39	40	41	42	17
8	TU	19	20	30	31	32	32	33	34	35	36	2	3	4	5	6	7	37	38	38	39	40	41	42	17
9	WE	18	19	20	30	31	32	32	33	34	35	36	2	3	4	5	6	7	30	31	32	33	34	35	16
10	TH	17	18	19	20	30	31	32	33	34	35	1	2	3	4	5	6	7	30	31	32	33	34	35	9
11	FR	10	11	12	13	14	30	31	32	33	34	35	1	2	4	5	6	7	30	31	32	32	33	34	35
12	SA	36	10	12	13	14	30	31	32	32	33	34	35	36	10	11	12	13	14	30	31	32	33	34	35
13	SU	9	10	11	12	13	14	30	31	32	33	34	35	9	10	11	12	13	14	22	23	24	25	26	27
14	MO	28	9	10	11	12	13	14	30	31	32	33	34	35	9	10	11	12	13	14	22	23	24	25	26	27
15	TU	28	1	2	3	4	5	6	7	37	38	39	40	41	9	10	11	12	13	14	22	23	24	25	26
16	WE	27	28	1	2	4	5	6	7	37	38	38	39	40	41	42	10	12	13	14	22	23	24	25	26
17	TH	27	28	1	2	3	4	5	6	7	37	38	38	39	40	41	42	17	18	19	20	22	23	24	25
18	FR	26	27	28	1	2	3	4	4	5	6	7	8	38	39	40	41	16	17	19	20	22	23	24	25
19	SA	25	26	27	28	29	2	3	4	4	5	6	7	8	38	39	40	41	16	17	19	20	22	23	24
20	SU	25	25	26	27	28	29	2	3	4	4	5	6	7	8	39	40	41	16	17	19	20	22	23	24
21	MO	24	25	25	26	27	28	29	2	3	4	4	5	6	7	8	38	38	39	40	41	42	17	19	20
22	TU	22	23	24	25	26	27	28	1	2	3	4	4	5	6	7	8	38	38	39	40	41	42	17	19
23	WE	20	22	23	24	25	26	27	28	1	2	3	4	5	6	7	30	31	32	33	34	35	9	10	11
24	TH	12	13	14	22	23	25	26	27	28	1	2	3	4	5	6	7	22	23	25	26	27	28	9	10
25	FR	11	12	13	14	22	23	25	26	27	28	1	2	4	5	6	7	22	23	24	25	26	27	28	1
26	SA	2	4	5	6	7	30	31	32	33	34	35	1	2	4	5	6	7	22	23	24	25	26	27	28
27	SU	1	2	4	5	6	7	30	31	32	33	34	35	1	2	4	5	6	7	22	23	25	26	27	28
28	MO	1	2	3	4	5	6	7	30	31	32	33	34	35	9	10	12	13	14	22	23	24	25	26	27
29	TU	28	1	2	3	4	5	6	7	30	31	33	34	35	9	10	11	12	13	14	22	23	24	25	26
30	WE	27	28	1	2	3	4	5	6	7	37	38	39	40	41	16	17	18	19	20	22	23	24	25	26

Chapter 5 for techniques for entering and leaving eddies in strong currents.) You may also improvise a route that forsakes the straight line to a destination and takes you veering off course to get into a giant back eddy that, although it increases your distance by 50 percent, cuts your travel time in half. Sometimes you just have to grin and paddle; it's not unusual in a single channel crossing to feel yourself alternately flying on favorable currents, then slowing to a crawl in suddenly opposing currents, and emerging ten minutes later on another escalator going your way. Anyone who says current predictions are a scientific matter hasn't spent enough time on the water.

There are, however, certain spots where you can count on strong, even dangerous, currents at times of maximum ebbs and maximum floods. You may not want to be in these places then, regardless of which direction you're headed. You'll just have to wait for slack water. If the location is well known, the current tables and certain charts will be quite explicit about the timing and strength of the current, including a prediction for the times of slack water: there are usually four per day, two occurring before flood currents and two before the ebbs.

Slack is defined as the moment when a current is stopped and is about to change its direction, but don't bet your boat on figuring that out on the basis of your visual observation as to when, say, low tide occurred. My source, Island Canoe Company's *Current and Tide Tables for Puget Sound, Deception Pass, Gulf Islands and Strait of Juan de Fuca,* says that "Because of variables, especially inertia (or 'slosh'), this moment [slack] does not usually correspond to the moment when tide is highest or lowest." Another expert says that it never corresponds; you need to rely on the current tables.

And a final reminder: like the tide tables, current predictions are made for a particular location and for subsidiary locations. You must make time and speed adjustments relative to the major reference points. Remember that the point of measurement may well be in a part of the channel that is used by big boats, not along the shoreline, which is where you are more likely to be traveling.

ELEMENTARY SEAMANSHIP (For Kayakers)

Among bush pilots, there is a saying to the effect that "there are old pilots, and there are bold pilots, but there are no old, bold pilots." The sea kayaker's environment is not quite so unforgiving, yet I have observed that there are strong paddlers, and there are smart paddlers. The best are both strong and smart. By strong I mean technically as well as physically strong. It is quite possible for the strong paddler to bully his or her way through an itinerary that *deals with,* rather than *plans around,* the problems that can arise. Windy, whitecapped waters, unfavorable currents, surf landings, or just plain long miles are taken in stride. Such paddlers may be a bit disappointed if the trip is uneventful in terms of sea states and the elements. Strong paddlers are not necessarily daredevils or mentally retarded thrill seekers; they usually have a very acute sense of their limits, and they enjoy testing them.

Smart paddlers have mastered the basic paddling skills and regard the sea kayaker's challenge as a mental rather than a physical game. Solid skills are the insurance for a well-planned and smartly executed "float plan." Persons who are inclined toward the smart approach to kayaking and who aspire to be top pilots and navigators should refer to *Fundamentals of Kayak Navigation* by David Burch, the definitive work on the subject. We can only scratch the surface of the subject here.

LEARNING SEAMANSHIP

The best way to learn the art and practice of seamanship is to travel with paddlers who are good at it. This can include commercially organized trips. If you are like most of us, there's a tendency to follow the leader unquestioningly, and unless that person is going to be your mentor, you may complete a trip without knowing why you did what you did. Ask questions about the route and get the trip leader to go over the chart with you to outline his or her navigational strategy. A thoughtful leader may provide photocopies of the applicable chart, and you should practice on your own as you go. Bring a compass and mark your chart; don't just follow the stern of the kayak in front of you. Even if the destination is clearly in view, keep track of your compass bearing and other land features to help fix your position. Constantly monitor drift caused by winds or currents. Keep track of time over distance; that will be a crucial element of planning and execution when you are on your own.

When you begin to plan your own trips, gather together numerous source materials, starting with a state road map. Nautical charts are so microfocused that it is possible for you to know the number of rocks in a certain tiny bay but not know what planet it's on. Use a large area map to get a sense of major geographic features, the general orientation of the body of water (which will give meaning to the wind and weather forecasts), and nearby points of civilization, including roads and highways.

Finding the right launching and landing spot is often the most important navigation you'll do. And you haven't even wetted your kayak yet! Guidebooks are your best source. Other paddlers—hopefully, ones who understand and respect property rights—often know of unpublicized or not-so-obvious launch spots. Public boat ramps can often be used, but, ironically, these have their own hazards, including the potential for getting in the way of a powerboater who may think you have no right being there. Even if it's a public

launch site, you *may not* belong there, at least not until you've paid your permit fee or obtained a "sticker."

Your guidebook, depending on its quality and level of detail, will usually provide a good general description of a trip, including distances, difficulty rating, crossing distances (if any), special hazards, and a nautical chart number. Often the guidebook will include both an access map—how to get to the launch—as well as a rough map of the trip area with a distance scale and highlights of its major features, such as tide rips, campsites, lighthouses, and points of interest. Such maps are often quite crude and should be used mainly for preliminary planning; chart your route on an actual nautical chart.

Magazine articles are another good source of trip descriptions, and if the magazine is specifically aimed at paddlers, like *Canoe* or *Sea Kayaker,* there are usually locator or area maps and lists of other resources, such as charts, outfitters, and specific guidebooks. Consider using *back* issues of magazines for your trip plans, or you may find you have lots of company.

Once you've decided on a trip destination, it's time to acquire your detailed nautical charts. If you are in an area where sea kayaking is popular, your best bet may be a paddlesports retailer: they usually have the guidebooks, and they may have specially formatted charts for the most popular destinations in your area. In Seattle, for example, the local retailers are likely to have coated, waterproof charts covering the North and South Puget Sound on the opposite sides of one chart; a chart covering all of the San Juan Islands; one for the neighboring Canadian Gulf Islands, and so on. These are less detailed and usually cover a little more territory than the nautical charts prepared by the NOAA. Large-scale, highly detailed charts are fun and often reveal more than you ever wanted to know, but over the years I've discovered the Murphy's law of charts: your area of travel will invariably encompass the corners of four separate nautical or topographical maps.

CHARTS

This section will deal primarily with the nautical charts produced by the NOAA and by the Canadian Hydrographic Service, but you can do general trip planning with the DeLorme state gazetteers for some coastal states, and even a good road map. Topographical maps prepared by the United States Coast and Geodetic Survey (USGS) are useful if you plan to probe inland, either by river travel or by hiking. They will show roads and trails in detail, and they can be a nice complement to the nautical charts. The "topos" are most useful in scales, 1:62,500 and 1:125,000 (that's roughly 1 or 2 miles to the inch). While topos are the best maps for land forms and features, the nautical charts also contain many representations of contours and other geographical features when they are either near the shoreline or are obvious reference points for piloting.

Piloting is, in fact, the term for navigation by landmark or navigational aids, such as buoys, channel markers, and lights. Take the word of this recreational navigator: fixing your position by identifying a navigation light is more comforting than counting off headlands, calculating your distance over time, and staying precisely on a compass bearing—all of which are subject to gross error. In general, the best strategy is to plot your course, follow the rules, and *then* rely on a number of piloting confirmations to ensure a safe and timely arrival.

There are a number of critical components in a nautical chart, and your familiarity with these will make them easy to decipher. These are:

- scale
- depth measurement
- chart symbols
- shoreline and land contours
- the compass rose

Scale

Nautical charts, Canadian and U.S., use a wide variety of scales; for example, 1:36,676; 1:40,000; 1:90,000; or no scale indicated at all. Most kayakers want to work with large-scale maps, which I will define as less than 1 mile to the inch. A common scale for Canadian waters is 1:40,000—an inch is about 6/10 of a mile (the smaller the number after the colon, the larger the scale). What's the ideal size? That depends. Sometimes charts are available only in one or two scales, and you want to balance your need for detail with the cost and clutter of too many large-scale maps. When you are covering long distances over many days, it makes sense to use the smallest possible scale while still showing the necessary detail. For certain coastlines, however, where the location and nature of safe landing areas is uncertain, you may want to acquire larger-scale maps. Regardless of the scale, the handiest and most useful element in a nautical chart is found along the vertical borders, where degrees and minutes of latitude are ticked off. (Latitude lines also extend across the chart at five-minute intervals.) All you need to know is that a minute of latitude equals 1 nautical mile. Better yet, make a handspan along the vertical border to get the number of miles to a handspan. (My handspan on a 1:40,000 chart is 5 miles—a nice round number.) In moments you can transfer your hand-

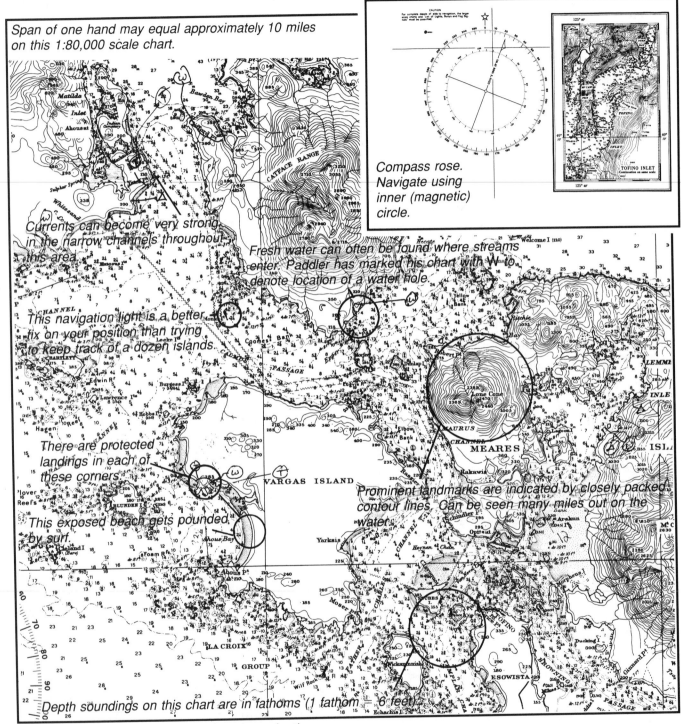

Span of one hand may equal approximately 10 miles on this 1:80,000 scale chart.

Compass rose. Navigate using inner (magnetic) circle.

Currents can become very strong in the narrow channels throughout this area.

Fresh water can often be found where streams enter. Paddler has marked his chart with W to denote location of a water hole.

This navigation light is a better fix on your position than trying to keep track of a dozen islands.

There are protected landings in each of these corners.

Prominent landmarks are indicated by closely packed contour lines. Can be seen many miles out on the water.

This exposed beach gets pounded by surf.

Depth soundings on this chart are in fathoms (1 fathom = 6 feet).

Chart showing some important clues to navigation.

span to your actual or intended routes or crossings and get a quick read on your overall route plan.

Depth Measurements

Normally referred to as *soundings,* depths are given on some charts in meters, and on others in a combination of fathoms and feet (1 fathom equals 6 feet). The chart will tell you which units it's using. You might find that soundings are more important for fishing than for navigation, but when it comes time to plan a route across a shallow bay or into an estuary, those little numbers can be critical. A broad, sandy beach offering an easy landing at low or mid-tide can become a steep embankment at high tide. The depths indicated on a chart are for low tide, so add the tide height from the tide tables to obtain the depth of water at high tide. You will also notice a color coding of the shoreline area on a chart: yellow-tan, green, and blue (or white). These colors indicate, respectively, land that is always dry, shore that uncovers as the tide ebbs, and areas that are always water.

Depth measurements also determine which rocks will be showing at various tide levels. The notations are rather confusing, but you are free to study and memorize them. Knowing when and where barely submerged rocks will appear at various tide levels is important for fast-moving, large craft, but in a kayak you can navigate on the fly. Your main concern with rocks should be of a more general nature. An area, either along the coast or in the middle of a channel, where there are many rocks is likely to be an area of considerable disturbance when wind and currents are swirling about them (see Chapter 6), and you may simply want to steer clear of such areas on all but the calmest days. In certain situations, depending upon water depth and the direction of wind and waves, they could also serve as an area of protection.

Chart Symbols

Get a copy of *Chart No. 1:* Symbols Abbreviations and Terms from any chart or map dealer. It's your key to deciphering the hundreds of dashes, slashes, shadings, and squiggles that you'll find all over your nautical chart. You will want particularly to familiarize yourself with the navigational danger symbols: rocks and rocky areas, tide rips, kelp or seaweed beds, and breakers. The other important symbols for coastal kayakers are those that describe the shore and foreshore, denoting rubble, sand, cliffs, rocks, mud, or a combination of these features. Finally, take special note of navigational aids such as lights. On a trip along an especially wild area on the west coast of British Columbia's Vancouver Island, I thought I had carefully counted off the headlands and the little bays and indentations. But my distance-over-time calculations were driven out of whack by hair-straightening head winds interspersed with short respites as we dashed behind protected points. We were headed for open ocean before my wife noticed a light shining from a rocky cliff. We had paddled right past the bay that was to be our refuge for the night. The next stop was Japan. It's easy to misread a coastal contour; a light is a positive identification.

Shoreline and Land Contours

As indicated earlier, *Chart No. 1* can help you interpret a coastline, but often you will need to paddle in close if you want to confirm a shoreline's suitability for landing. Binoculars are useful

CHART NO. 1
UNITED STATES OF AMERICA

NAUTICAL CHART
Symbols Abbreviations and Terms

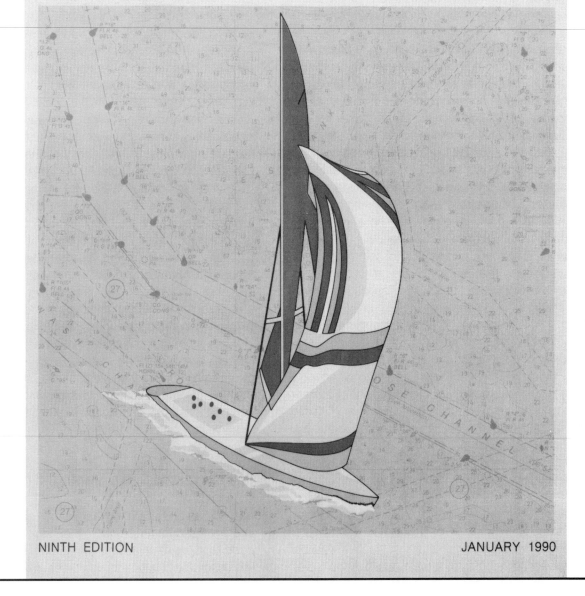

NINTH EDITION

JANUARY 1990

for this purpose. Contour maps, on the other hand, can be very handy for planning and piloting. Nautical charts are not so detailed as topo maps in displaying land formations, but the chartmakers know that coastal travelers need fixed and distinguishable landmarks by which to navigate. So steep cliffs, a notable peak or pinnacle, even a half-mile-long island with a 100-foot-high pimple on it will be shown on the chart. Check the contour interval. If the interval is 50 feet and an island is depicted with four concentric contour lines, you've got a 200-foot bump—or point, or whatever—on the island. Closely packed contours indicate steep terrain. As you look down a coastline or across a channel to a group of islands and discern an almost undifferentiated mass of land, your chart may show that one or more of the points or distant islands has hills or a high promontory. These can be the objective upon which you set your compass course. Major features such as the "Family Humps" (see page 86), can be seen from the water from many miles and many directions. With such features in sight you are able to fix your general, or precise, position, no matter how confusing your immediate surroundings may be.

The Compass Rose

Even if you failed your merit-badge test for the map and compass in the Scouts, don't despair. The compass rose (see inset page 86) found on all nautical charts makes route planning simple for coastal kayakers. True north (how the mapmaker sees the world) and magnetic north (how your compass sees the world) can differ substantially—a 20-degree difference would not be unusual in some of our northern coastal areas. What's important to the coastal kayaker is magnetic north, and the inner circle on the compass

rose is all you need to be concerned with. Take a pencil and draw a straight line from your present point to your objective, say, an island 3 miles distant. Use a set of parallel rulers or a 5-by-7-inch note card to determine the corresponding (parallel) line through the center of the compass rose. The point on your compass rose (the inner circle) where your ruler (or card) intersects gives you your compass course. You can buy extra compass roses to stick on your charts to make it even easier to transfer your parallel lines. Under way in a kayak, you can use a paddle shaft as your ruler for a quick-and-dirty course setting, but you should try to plan as much of your route as possible before you set out. In the comfort of your living room, with the map spread out on the floor, take a pencil and ruler and make a bunch of lines for any number of possible routes. Get your degree readings off the rose and write them next to your lines. You might even wish to put two numbers on each line: your outbound course (say, 270 degrees) and its reciprocal (90 degrees, or 270 minus 180) for the return route.

On the water, you may find that you want to take a different route than the one you laid out on your chart. Often a rough interpolation will be close enough for your purposes. Unless you are into some very complicated and extended tripping, you will find that most of your navigation is a matter of general directions and coastal landmarks. Of course, trying to hit a small island 6 miles distant and obscured by fog is another matter.

THE TOOLS

Of course, the chart and the chart symbols are your primary tools. Some additional paste-on compass roses would also be useful. A set of parallel rulers or a draftsman's square with transparent Lucite edges make easy work of drawing courses on your chart. A waterproofing agent, such as Map Seal, which you simply paint onto your chart, is a good idea, and you can still make notations on your map with a china marker. You can also use a ballpoint pen, if you don't mind marking up your map permanently. Cut the superfluous white border off your chart; you may also want to cut one large chart into two or more smaller charts for easier handling. A clear plastic chart case, about 20 by 27 inches, with grommets in each corner and a zipper at one end, is ideal for carrying your working chart on deck. You can attach plastic snap clips to the grommets and snap these to the deck rigging guides in front of your cockpit. Ideally, you will be able to unfold the map case to flop your chart right on top of your spray skirt. When you're trying to count off headlands and identify passing islands and lights, you want the map on deck and visible—but it can't be flapping in the wind or obstructing your paddle stroke.

Don't forget the compass. It's an essential item for safety, and for fun. There really is no substitute for a deck-mounted compass, though many kayakers have fared well for years with a simple orienteering compass. They keep it in their pocket or on a string around their neck while on land and set it on deck when they're afloat. A deck-mounted compass *and* a pocket compass is the way I like to travel. Get in the habit of reading your compass bearing on even the simplest of routes and be especially conscious of the ease with which you slip off of a straight-line course.

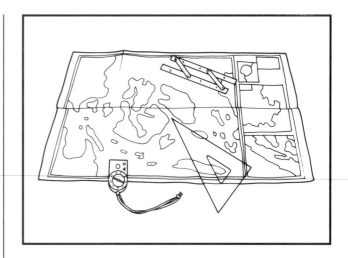

Rulers and compass for marking up your chart with possible routes

You can set your general direction using the sun, wind, and waves as your guide, but check your compass occasionally; your senses can be fooled. It's no big deal when your objective is clearly in view, but on a foggy crossing you'll appreciate knowing which rudder pedal to push to regain the 5-degree slippage off course that occurs due to inattentiveness or the random swell. In rough water, holding a steady course is a special challenge.

In waters subject to currents, pay particular attention to your compass bearing. On a clear day, you might find that during a 3-mile channel crossing your compass reading keeps changing. Let's say you shoved off toward an island on a heading of 350 degrees, but halfway across the channel you note that your compass now reads 320 degrees, despite the fact that the nose of your kayak is pointed directly at the same prominent landmark you were originally heading for. Your kayak has drifted, or been "set," in an easterly direction (see page 91). Obviously, if you had

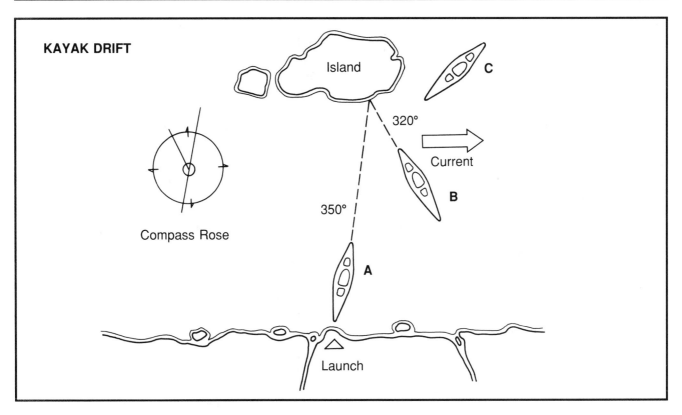

KAYAK DRIFT

Island

C

320°

Current

B

350°

A

Compass Rose

Launch

*Boat launched on course of 350°; set by current to
320°. Boat **C** stayed on constant bearing of 350°,
and missed island.*

stayed on a constant bearing of 350, you'd have
missed the island, just like boat C. That can happen in the fog. But fog or no fog, a boat that must
continually change its heading to reach its objective—especially on a long crossing—will end up
taking a long, elliptical course, expending more
energy than necessary. We'll look at some tricks
to deal with fog and currents later in the chapter.

At this point, it's worth defining a few of the
terms that I have already sprinkled around. Your
course is your intended line of travel—for example, from the launch in the figure on page 91 to

the bluff on the island. Your *heading* is the direction in which the boat is pointed. The compass
bearing is the direction to a particular landmark.
They can all be the same, but for our current-
driven paddler in the figure, they keep changing
as he paddles toward his bluff.

SOME TRICKS

There is no substitute for practice. The more time you spend on the water, the more capable a pilot and navigator you will become. In time you will become a better judge of distances and of your own travel speed, better at correlating actual land features to the contours on your chart, and better at developing tactics for dealing with currents. That's why it's important to practice navigation on your simplest routes, where there is complete visibility, known distances, and known landmarks. As a whitewater paddler might say, "Practice Class III moves on Class II water before moving to the next level of difficulty."

There are a few tricks to help solve several of the most common navigational problems that occur even on relatively modest outings.

Dead Reckoning

Here's a term you've undoubtedly heard. The *dead* is really *ded,* as in *deduced.* You deduce your position by observing the amount of time since you left a known point and guessing (or knowing) your speed. If you paddle at 3 knots and you've been on the water for twenty minutes on a constant compass heading, you have obviously gone 1 nautical mile. But it is obvious *only* if you know precisely that you are making 3 knots over the water. Head winds, tail winds, currents, and the few minutes you took to clean off your sunglasses can all foul up this simplest of arithmetic. So it's important that you first do the kayaker's version of time trials to get a good sense of your paddling speed. Time yourself on any normal trip or set your own trials mission. You need a long enough distance to allow for some fatigue; you need to be carrying the sort of load you would

normally have on a trip; and you have to be on a stretch of water devoid of current or wind. The distance between your two "trial" points must be known. Most kayak tourists travel at 3 to 4 knots, so if your time trial produces a much higher or lower result, make sure you followed the rules and did your arithmetic correctly.

And that's the easy part. In actual paddling conditions, wind and currents, even fatigue from your all-night drive to the put-in, can affect your speed. Your allowance for such factors will be largely guesswork, but, based upon some empirically measurable forces, you can get pretty close. If you know (from current tables), or can guess the speed of the current, you may reasonably calculate that in (add or subtract) to your flatwater paddling speed. Wind is a tougher bit of guesswork, and tail winds don't help you anywhere near as much as head winds hold you back. For example, a paddler who averages 3 knots on flat water will be slowed to 2 knots in a 15-knot head wind (a 30-percent degradation), but he would be lucky to gain half a knot in a tail wind of the same velocity. The relationship worsens as winds increase above that.

Where wind and currents are in opposition, as winds increase beyond 10 knots, the current speed necessary to offset your headwind may be a moot point. Rough water and stability will be your concern by the time current speed theoretically overcomes wind force. Forget the theories; there is no such thing as a good head wind.

These are neat things to know—and much has been left out of the equation—but your own experience and time on the water is the only true path to dead-reckoning accuracy. Until you have paddled your own loaded boat into a 15-knot head wind and calculated your speed between two known points, all the graphs, tables, and force-pound theories in the world won't tell you where you are.

The Ferry

This paddling maneuver is described in Chapter 5. Its purpose as a navigational maneuver is to get you across a channel with a strong current, without your getting set off your course in the manner of boat C (see page 91). In the figure below, the paddler maintains a constant *course* of 350 degrees, but his *heading* may be a constant 300 degrees. In a very strong current, he might have to maintain a heading of 280 degrees. As mentioned earlier, simply keeping your nose pointed at your destination and paddling hard, will cause you to take the longer, elliptical route B (see below).

In most real-life channel crossings, the currents will vary as you make your way across and you may have to adjust your boat angle. In general, the stronger the current, the more you have to point your kayak into the current to get ferried across. It's as much art, or feel, as science.

Reverse Azimuth

Terminology again: an azimuth is simply a compass bearing line, such as 350 degrees. The reverse azimuth trick is a variation of the ferrying scheme described above but it permits you to adjust your ferry angle, or heading, when you can't

---

Kayaker maintains heading of 300° to stay on course A of 350°. Course B is likely route if paddler keeps bow pointed at island.

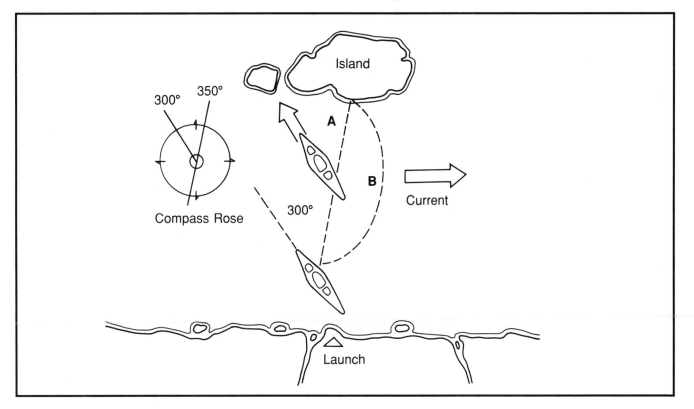

see the opposite shore, in what's called a "blind crossing." Suppose you are the kayaker in the figure on page 93, starting out in thick fog. You know, or guess, that there is a good current in excess of 2 knots and you make a further guess that a heading of 300 degrees will set you on the course you want. After paddling for five minutes, maintaining your 300-degree heading, you can still see your launch point. If your guess was correct, your launch point should be at 170 (350 degrees minus 180) or the "reverse" of your plotted course. You check your compass and see that the point where you launched is instead at 180. You are being set an additional 10 degrees off your course by a current stronger than you guessed. You must adjust your heading by 10 degrees, to 310, to compensate. Practice this on a clear day!

Aiming Off

This is an orienteer's trick and is perfect for the imperfect world of the kayak navigator. Call it a calculated error. It's no way to find an island, but suppose you want to paddle from the island to the launch point. Except it isn't your launch point; it's a beach campsite—and the only one—on a coast you've never seen before. You plot your course: 170 degrees, naturally, and you do a superb job of staying on course despite winds, currents, rough seas, and intermittent thick fog. Upon arrival at the far side, there is nothing but a steep, rock-bound shoreline stretching in either direction. No sign of the bay containing your beach. Which direction do you go? You have a 50 percent chance of going the wrong way.

No matter how carefully you plot your course, it's easy to go astray—a degree or two will put you in the predicament described above. And the longer your crossing, the greater the likelihood and amount of error. The solution is to "aim off";

that is, to plot a course of travel that is as much as 5 degrees off the direct, straight-line route. You are *planning* on making an error to put you to the east of your objective. When you hit the opposite shore, you have only one choice: turn right and paddle up the shore until you find your bay. The paddler who attempted to follow course A (at right), the direct route, could easily have gone off course and been on course B due to current drift.

This is not intended to be a chapter of intimidation. Yes, there's a lot more to navigation than has been covered here in simplified form, and sometimes the mariner's lingo seems to be designed to confuse the uninitiated. The fact is that the vast majority of your day trips will not require much in the way of navigation to get you where you want to be. You'll be following a shoreline until you get to your destination; you'll paddle back again. But you don't need to be Christopher Columbus to practice and master some of these basic concepts, and it turns out that it's fun. If you are like me, you grew up imagining yourself as a pilot and navigator on the mighty ocean. With a small boat, a chart, and a $25 compass, you can start learning the lingo and the tricks that those yacht- and shipmasters have been mystifying us with for years.

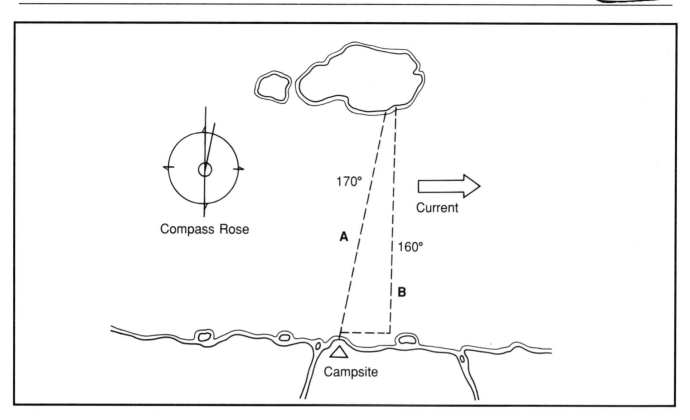

170°

Compass Rose

Current

A

160°

B

Campsite

*Paddler leaves island on a 165° heading, is set to
east 5°, and has an actual course of 160°. Paddler
must turn west upon reaching shore to find his bay.*

CHAPTER 9

SURF LANDING

The last three chapters were about the sea kayaker's environment, ways to get around in it, and how to deal with its idiosyncrasies and avoid its worst moods. I've left this chapter for late in the book to convey the message that surf landings should be something of a last resort. There may come a time, however, when your options are limited and getting into an exposed beach is necessary. There are some strategies, as well as some boat-handling techniques, that can enhance your chances of a safe landing while sparing your boat.

Surf kayaking is an exhilarating sport of its own, but it is done in short, specialized "skis" or whitewater kayaks that are suited to the task. A loaded sea kayak is the worst possible vehicle for negotiating surf. It's too long and almost impossible to turn when your nose or tail is buried in a leading or pursuing wave. When the wave that is propelling you forward, nose down, collapses, you will almost surely be broached. If the wave that collapsed under you doesn't finish you off, the next one will. As ominous as this sounds, you can take some measures to ensure a greater chance of success.

Your first problem is that from seaward you are at a poor vantage for judging the actual severity of the breakers. If there is a "line," you are poorly positioned to see either the route or rocks, reefs or logs between you and the shore. All you see are the smoothly retreating backs of the waves as they roll toward the beach. But let's assume you have no choice but to take an unfamiliar beach head on. Here are a few ideas:

Let the strongest member of your group—presumably one who has some skill and experience in making a surf landing—go in first. Once on the beach, he is in a position to give signals to the rest of the party and even direct their route. He should be able to judge when the sets are the least severe and give the "go" signal when they mellow. He can motion the following paddlers in a direction where there may be a smoother line. Maybe the most valuable role for those who have landed is to grab the bow of their comrades' boats as they rush the beach and drag them up the beach before the next wave hits. This is a helpful gesture in gentle surf as well.

It's usually not wise to simply rush the beach. Rather, sit comfortably off shore for a while to get a feel for timing the sets. You'll discern a pattern and a time when the period lengthens and the magnitude of the waves passing under you diminishes. If a wave begins to lift you before you are ready, back paddle, and the wave will pass under you. You don't want to get picked up and be launched shoreward before you're ready. Suppose you just plain miscalculate (a high probability) and you do, in fact, get picked up and hurled at the beach. As you rocket toward impact, you feel your kayak sluing around to broach to the next incoming wave. You must quickly cock your boat hard to seaward and plant a high brace on the top of the froth of the breaking wave. Unless it is truly a dumper, it will support you. Hang out on your brace until the soup leaves you on the sand, and be ready to get out of the boat quickly. It's not likely that you will stay dry, but you will have been mostly, if inelegantly, in control.

Another strategy for landing when you have no other option, is to approach the beach fully prepared to broach and brace. This permits you to go in at somewhat of an angle, such that you know you will be broached on to a right-side brace—assuming that's your strong side.

THE UN-SURF LANDING

Practicing the moves described above on a sandy beach, on a warm day, and in an empty boat is a good idea; then you'll have the planned broach-and-brace in your arsenal for that day when there's no other choice. But even when your options seem limited, take careful note of the shape of the beach and the direction of the swell. In the figure at right (below), the kayaker has rightly surmised that the swell can't get around the corner and he's found a sneak route for a relatively stress-free landing. When you are in an expensive kayak, filled with expensive equipment, there's no need for heroics.

Other features in a bay pounded by surf may also give you a reprieve. A cluster of rocks may provide a natural breakwater; you can go around and behind them to find quieter water washing up on the beach. Or there may be some tiny pocket beaches within a larger embayment. Often, these are defined by a narrow rocky entrance. Kelp beds may also break up the incoming swell. Needless to say, whether rocks or kelp, you don't want to get surfed into their clutches; you want to get between their protective matrix and the beach.

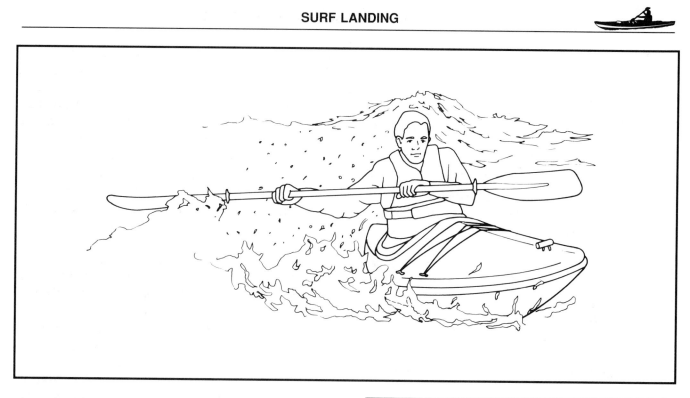

Lean into the wave on your high or low brace (low brace shown here).

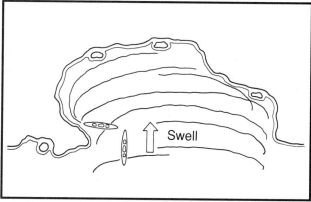

Sneaking in behind the point. The swell can't turn the corner.

LAUNCHING

Unlike in a landing, where your line and possible obstacles are obscured from view by the waves, from the shore not only can you find the quietest stretch of beach to launch, but often, a path or line to take you beyond the surf zone will be visible to you. This may be an area of deep water or a break in a reef or reeflike obstruction that is creating the buildup of surf. As with a landing situation, you should be watching and monitoring the sets to find the pattern and the time when the wave height decreases. Launching into the surf, like landing, can be aided by a companion. Once you are organized in your kayak, spray skirt secure and paddle at the ready, he or she can line you up—directly perpendicular to the incoming waves—and slide you down the beach with a mighty push to sea; then, you paddle like blazes.

As with landing, your launch, too, should take account of the wave sets; the larger waves will wash farther up the beach, and recede farther. Wait for the smaller waves in the set, getting into your kayak during the low part of the set. Then, wait for perhaps four to ten waves and be prepared to shove off as the bigger waves come up to where you are on the beach. Your challenge will be to avoid getting turned sideways before your launch has some seaward momentum. Also consider timing your launch with the sets to go out on big waves in a dumping surf and small waves in spilling surf.

Many steep and gravelly beaches lend themselves to an easier self-launch than is possible on a sloping beach. A steeper beach or one with the kind of gravel that works like ball bearings on the bottom of a kayak, will allow you to get completely organized in your kayak, the paddle across the cockpit in front of you; then, reach down and launch yourself into the surf using your hands as propulsion. You can actually lift up the hull of your kayak with your sitting push-up. The trick, once you've pushed yourself to sea, is to grab that paddle as soon as you hit real water and start paddling with vigor. If you've got a sturdy paddle, you can use it to do your push-off.

All of this assumes that the surf problems are right at the beach launch site—that is, that the waves are approaching a beach that slopes in a consistent incline from deeper water offshore to shallower water at the landing. Life is not always so simple. In certain surf conditions, your visual observation will suggest that you adopt the pot-of-tea-and-book strategy discussed earlier. A tougher decision may be required when the surf or the compression of waves on an offshore reef or a beach anomaly are some distance out; in other words, your launch may be relatively uneventful, but within 25 or 50 yards (or more) you may face formidable surf. Waves in excess of 6 feet in height may be the practical limit for AHBs ("average human beings"—a coinage of some outdoor writer), but how do you judge? David Seidman, writing in *Canoe* magazine, suggests that you stand on the beach at a point estimated to be the same height as the wave troughs. If you are 6 feet tall and the tops of the waves appear to rise above the horizon line, they are over 6 feet in height. Kneel (4 feet) or sit (2 feet), and you've got a fair approximation of wave height.

Even a high-breaking wave can be penetrated or ridden up and over. You need good forward speed and a direct (90-degree) angle of attack. As you start to ascend the wave face, apply power to keep your speed up. If your timing is off, or if the wave is steeper than you figured, you have to present the lowest profile possible. Get your nose close to the deck, keep your paddle low, and be completing a forward power stroke (which will align your paddle with the boat) as the wave passes under, over, or "through you." You should be pulling water hard and keep pulling until you are sure you have gone beyond the surf zone. As you might guess, "through you" is not to be desired. No matter what else, don't let the wave hit you full in the chest, and don't have your paddle shaft any higher than your belly button. The ocean throws a powerful punch. Duck it, and then swing those blades like your life depended on it. (It just might!)

WAITING FOR THE MOMENT

Every scenario described above represents a real-life situation that I have dealt with, from Hawaii to the mainland coast to Lake Superior. But virtually all of those situations, save Hawaii, were contrived—that is, I was training, testing, or otherwise doing research to prepare for that moment when I might need some tricks in my bag. You should do the same if you want to get beyond the standard tours. Let's call it a form of insurance. Otherwise, do what wise mariners usually do: work at planning, chart reading, and the execution of a conservative trip plan that eliminates, as much as possible, the kind of risks that surf landings and launchings can involve.

10

TRIP PLANNING AND PACKING

Making a living and getting the shutters painted are facts of life for most of us; there's never enough time, and our kayak trips tend to get crammed into a day or a long weekend—usually on the nearest available piece of water. The fact is, you can learn and practice most of the skills discussed in this book in your nearby venues. Weekend outings, paddling on long summer evenings, and the occasional day of hooky are a few ways to keep the paddling muscles tuned as well. They are also a time to imagine yourself probing the Florida Keys, whale watching in Baja, or exploring the fjords of the Labrador coast. I have prepared for and planned a hundred trips I've never taken.

This book has been written and the chapters presented, hopefully, in a manner which leads you up to the point where you are ready to load the kayaks on your van and head for open water, somewhere. You want to be out for a week or a month. The good news is that anytime you plan and pack for a trip with even one overnight, you'll follow the same organizational process and deal with the same gear list. The only difference is the amount of food. Yes, a two-week coastal journey might demand that you include a repair kit, emergency rations, a bigger map case, and so on, but the basic outfit will be the same. The bad news is that your short trips usually involve a disproportionate time of "fiddling" to actual paddling. That's a good reason to set the goal of taking one long trip a year. Anyway, isn't that one of the reasons we learned to read a tide table and navigate on a reverse azimuth?

This chapter is not *everything* you'll ever need to know about going camping in a kayak. It is, rather, a discussion of some of the special requirements of the kayaker—as compared to, say, the backpacker or the canoe tripper—due to both the nature of the coastal environment and the craft itself.

THE PLAN

Chapters 6, 7, and 8 set forth the many elements of the coastal and open-water environment, along with some tools for dealing with that environment—but how do you put it all together into a trip plan? Sometimes a guidebook or a magazine article or another kayaker's trip description will lay out a route for you. But this is *your* trip. It must be designed around your time, physical stamina, skills and the makeup of your paddling crew. (Your trip must, in fact, be planned around the weakest member of the party, and that's not meant disparagingly. He or she may be a non-paddling six-year-old who will be traveling in the center hatch of a double.) Whether your trip is near or far, and especially if you are the trip organizer, fill out a float plan and leave it with a friend, relative, or coworker. A sample plan, provided to us by L.L. Bean, a major outdoor retailer, can be found in the Appendix.

There are basically three trip plans: the base camp, the out-and-back (or circular), and the point-to-point, listed in order of potential complexity. Let's look at the most ambitious first. You might want to paddle a portion of the Maine Island Trail, starting in Wiscasset and ending in Castine. Your itinerary would include stops in small harbors (like Camden or Rockport), rough camps on small islets, an overnight at a bed-and-breakfast, and a side trip deep into the Penobscot River estuary. You may want to see and photograph a dozen lighthouses along the way. Such a trip would demand a high level of boating and navi-

gational skills. You'll have to have a good sense of your daily mileage capabilities; you'll have to be able to find escape routes or alternate campsites if weather alters your itinerary and be knowledgeable and prepared for any eventuality. You will be setting and breaking camp almost every day, so you'll have to be well organized when it comes to packing and unpacking the boats. Your mileage calculations must make provision for the time consumed by breaking camp and getting on the water.

Going point-to-point has the greatest potential for truly getting yourself out on a limb. And you have to set up a shuttle system to connect Wiscasset (the put in) and Castine (the takeout), since you are now in Castine with a kayak and the car is back at the put in. For a ten-day itinerary, you had better budget four additional days to allow for weather delays. A nonrefundable deposit on a room at the Pentagoet Inn in Castine for day ten could be a bad investment at best, or, at worst, an invitation to tragedy, if you chance a storm in order to keep the rendezvous. That said, the point-to-point odyssey is something to dream about; you maximize the variety of landfalls and seascapes, and you are assured a memorable adventure.

Going out and back is the more common trip plan, but it carries some of the same risks as the point-to-point format. Like the point-to-point, you have an opportunity to maximize the variety of scenery, but in the case of a circular itinerary, your outbound route may serve as an alternate return route, since you will be able to familiarize yourself with its hazards and its refuges as you go. Some circular routes may include an inside (that is, protected) line and an outside line (exposed to open ocean). Inbound or outbound, you can choose the route depending on wind and weather, taking the exposed route when favorable conditions prevail, sneaking inside when conditions deteriorate. The logistics of access and egress are simple: your van is waiting at the put-in.

For beginning voyagers, and for a more relaxed plan, the base camp is the best approach. A series of base camps is recommended for trips longer than a week; this also ensures that you aren't "hogging" a campsite that other parties may wish to use. A base-camp plan is definitely the answer for larger groups with a wide range of energy and skill levels. The amount of packing and unpacking is minimized. Everybody can get comfortable and know there's a safe harbor at day's end. For those who would really rather work on their suntan or read a good book, they can stay in camp while the Leif Erikssons in the group paddle off to a distant island, hike to the top of a volcano, or come back to camp with a hatch full of lingcod. If they're good guys, the "camp potatoes" will also have the pot on the fire when the expeditioners return.

Regardless of which format you choose, mileage is a common element in all of the plans. Randall Washburne (a favorite source of mine) has said that a kayaker's mileage is mostly a function of how long he's willing to sit in a kayak. Your butt and your bladder are almost as important a determinant of mileage as your aerobic and muscular capabilities. Unless you are traveling alone or in a tiny group of very strong paddlers, a 3-knot paddling speed is a reasonable planning tool. A 10-mile day is often more than enough for most groups, and it can be a very long day if wind and current slow the average speed to 2 knots. There is more to a crossing than just distance—currents, ship traffic, funneling winds, open-water boredom, and no beach to wash up on. When the time required to make a crossing approaches and exceeds an hour, you've got the potential for problems. In planning a crossing, consider how quickly the weather and currents can change for the worse. Know yourself and your crew. It is a gross oversimplification, but nonetheless true, to say that a trip honestly planned around the weakest paddler and the longest exposed crossing is the plan that will keep you out of trouble.

Group size, regardless of skill levels, is a major factor in planning mileage. Once your number exceeds four, there's an inverse (and possibly exponential) relationship between size and speed of group travel. The makeup of your crew is even more important than equipment. For a three-day trip you can usually deal with the whiners and complainers and compensate for an incapable member of the group. With each additional day you plan to be out, the need for good crew chemistry and overall paddling and camping competence increases. If you have a choice in paddling companions between one with a good sweep stroke and one with common sense, go for the latter.

CAMP CRAFT AND EQUIPMENT

We'll assume you have some basic camping skills, can start a fire in the rain, and aren't scared of the dark. If you have the basics for backpacking, you are virtually set, but you can leave out the backpack itself; your kayak is a backpack on the water. To give you an idea of what a sea kayaker might put in his floating backpack, check out the gear list on pages 106–107. The list is an amalgam of lists I've borrowed from others and there's enough on it for a summer-long expedition. You might want to substitute a ukulele for the repair kit if you are only on a three-day cruise on a nearby reservoir.

EQUIPMENT CHECKLIST

Boat Accessories

Paddle and spare
Spray skirt
Life jacket (PFD)
Bilge pump
Sponge
Painter (bowline)
Flotation
Storage bags
Paddle float bag or sponsons
Rope for rescues, stirrup
Sea anchor
Sail or kit

Navigational Equipment

Charts and map case
Current and tide tables
Compass
Binoculars
Weather radio

Repair Kit

Duct tape
Soft wire
Pliers
Light oil, WD-40
Swiss Army knife
Fiberglass patch kit (cloth, resin, catalyst)
Hull patch kit (for folding boats)

Emergency Equipment

Flares or signaling device
Emergency Position Indicating Radio
Beacon (EPIRB)
VHF or CB transmitter

Survival Equipment

Wet suit or dry suit
Whistle
Waterproof matches and fire starter
High-energy food bars
Tea or bouillon
Personal shelter (tarp, space blanket, etc.)

First-Aid Kit

Painkiller
Seasickness pills
Ace bandage
Sterile compresses
Gauze roll
Butterfly closures
Triangular bandages
Adhesive tape
Safety pins
Fast-acting laxative and emetic
Aspirin
Antibiotics
Burn ointment
Tweezers
Scissors
First-aid book

Clothing

Fast-drying pants (extra pair)
Wool or pile pants
Long underwear
Polypropylene undershirt
Wool or pile shirt
Sweater
Vest (synthetic fill)
Wool or pile hat
Broad-brimmed rain hat
Rain parka and pants
Paddling gloves or mitts (pogies)
Rubber boots (wading height)
Sandals, footwear for walking ashore

Camping Equipment

Tent and fly
Rain tarp
Sleeping bag, plus stuff and waterproof bag
Sleeping mat
Towel
Lighter or matches
Saw and small ax
Insect repellent
Toilet paper
Flashlight
Candles or lantern
Toilet kit
Sun shower
Dry bags for clothing and equipment
Mesh duffel and tote bags
Camera bag or box
Fishing gear

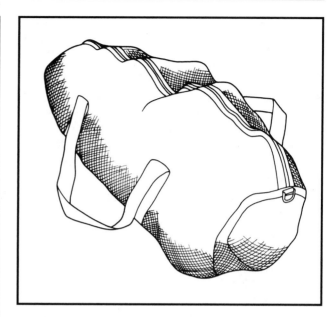

Mesh bags are great for consolidating little packs and carrying wet gear.

Cooking Equipment

Cook kit, pans, dutch oven
Stove and fuel
Eating and serving utensils
Dish soap and scrubbers
Cup
Spices
Food storage bags
Water containers (large and personal)
Water purifier

The kayaker's environment is wet, so plan accordingly. If you don't want a piece of gear, clothing, or your food getting wet, get waterproof bags for everything, and in a variety of sizes and shapes. Those with roll-up enclosures and a fastex buckle are relatively inexpensive and easy to open and close. The most important piece of gear to keep dry is your sleeping bag; use your stuffsack for stuffing; then, put your stuffed bag in a waterproof bag you can trust.

Unlike canoe trippers, who consolidate gear into as few packs as possible to facilitate portaging, the kayaker wants as many little packages as possible, enabling him to fill all the nooks and crannies of the boat. You won't be doing much portaging in the open-water environment, but you still have to get your mound of little packs to and from the kayak and from the beach to campsite. Invest in half a dozen high-volume mesh bags. You can then fill the mesh bags with smaller packs, as well as items like gum boots, PFDs, rod cases, bilge pumps, or a plastic coffee filter. The mesh bags are also great for transporting wet gear.

When you start loading hatches with gear, you are also changing the shape of your kayak's hull. A shakedown cruise with a fully loaded kayak pays off in a lot of ways, but getting the feel of how your loaded kayak paddles can eliminate some unpleasant surprises later on. How your boat is trimmed will make a difference in how it performs in various water conditions. See Lee Moyer's article "Stuff It!" which has been reprinted from *Canoe* magazine on page 109. It contains some good ideas on how to pack your gear as well. Here are some additional thoughts: your kayak floor is a cold place. If there are food containers, beverages, or other things you want to keep cold, take advantage of your natural refrigeration. Keep metal pots, the ax, ammo cans, and the like away from your deck mounted compass. These will cause compass deviation and make a shambles of your navigation efforts.

It's popular to worry about bears and food, but your most likely competition for calories will be critters like raccoons, chipmunks, and crows. What works for these bandits probably works for bears, because it puts the food—or, more precisely, the food smell—into quarantine. Pull your kayak up as close to your kitchen as you can; the hatches become your cupboard.

Canoe trippers and backpackers use them, but for the kayak tourer they are an absolute necessity: a good tarp and lots of cord. Whether it's the endless rains that might find the sea kayaker holed up for days (we do operate in a maritime climate, after all) or the unrelenting sun that draws us to the beach, a well-pitched tarp can make the difference between a good trip and a disaster.

Stuff It!

How to Load and Trim a Sea Kayak

by Lee Moyer

How a sea kayak handles is very sensitive to how the load is balanced or "trimmed" fore to aft. Some kayaks work so well when empty yet change their personalities when loaded. Adverse trim effects due to loading or design deficiencies can be rectified with a rudder. But if the rudder is working hard, it is producing considerable drag. It's better to trim the kayak properly.

Proper trim is not obvious. Setting a kayak on the floor and marking each end for a reference line will not necessarily produce a level trim line. Eyeballing the deck profile also is misleading since some kayaks are styled to have rakish appearance, others to have a minimum end profile. If one assumes the kayak is properly balanced on the water when paddled empty, the best way to establish a level reference trim line is to mark the actual waterline while the paddler sits in the kayak in calm water. Then, by marking and labelling increments above the noted waterline it is easy to see if the loaded kayak is still balanced.

Compared to level trim, bow-heavy trim produces a lower bow and higher stern. At the bow, this reduces the area exposed to the wind and increases the keel effect below the waterline. At the stern, the effect is just the opposite. As you paddle forward in a cross wind, the wind will blow the stern downwind while the bow stays securely anchored by its deeply entrenched keel. A bow-heavy kayak thus turns into the wind. Interestingly, a bow-heavy kayak with no hull speed will drift sideways to the wind and at high hull speeds the cross wind has less effect. The problem is most noticeable just below cruise speed. Bow-heavy trim also causes strong oversteer and makes control difficult even in good conditions.

Due to convenience and ignorance, most kayaks are paddled stern-heavy. Stern-heavy trim makes the kayak track very well in calm water, run easily with waves and surf, and resist pointing into the wind. Unless the weather gets bad, paddlers in stern-heavy kayaks won't know any better and assume they are properly trimmed. When the wind kicks up, you can identify these paddlers by their colorful vocabulary and desperate backstrokes as their kayak seems determined to run downwind into a problem.

One way to help achieve a well-balanced load is to divide all the cargo into three equal-sized piles, with the lightest stuff in one pile, the heaviest in another, and the leftovers in the third. Load the leftovers (about a third of the total) into the bow, the lightest pile into the stern toward the end of the kayak, and the heaviest last into the stern, close to the center of the kayak. You'll modify this system as experience shows how the kayak handles and whether you really have time to unload most of the gear to get to the toilet paper.

It's best to establish a consistent loading pattern so the kayak is always predictable, rather than arranging the load for the expected conditions. The conditions change faster than the paddler can rearrange the gear for optimum trim. On a double kayak trim is primarily a function of the paddlers' weights. You can use the gear load to help compensate for a weight difference but with the extra power of two paddlers, the speed and tracking of a longer hull and the control a rudder offers, trim is less of an issue on doubles than on singles. ∎

BRUCE MORSER

LIGHTEST HEAVIEST   LEFTOVERS

Reprinted from *Canoe* magazine, July, 1991

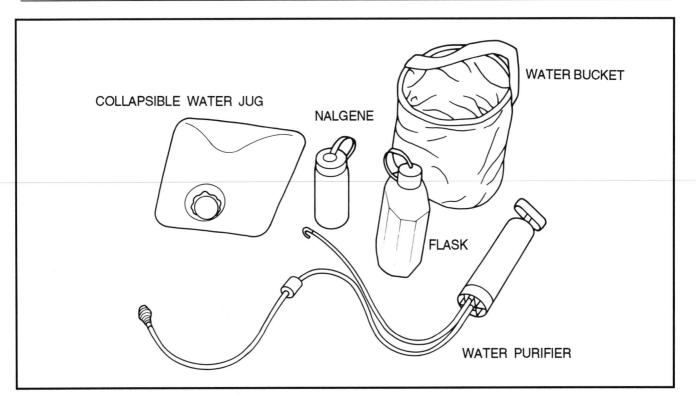

You'll need tools for gathering, transporting, and purifying fresh water in many areas.

WATER SUPPLY

Sea kayaking may be a wet sport, but keeping a good supply of fresh, potable water can be a challenge. There are many areas, especially if you go island hopping, where you'll have to carry your own supply. It is not unusual for an itinerary to include side trips to either civilization or a freshwater source in the wild (a creek or a spring) for the sole purpose of replenishing your supply.

Carry folding water containers, even a folding bucket. You'll also want four to six one-quart-size Nalgene bottles for gathering and for your personal quaff enroute. If you are going to be relying on rivers or creeks, carry a water purifier. Chemical treatment, such as with iodine and/or chlorine, and boiling are suitable defenses against such diseases as giardiasis, but you'll find many excellent mechanical purifiers on the market (including some with chemical elements) that work better and give you good-tasting water at the same time.

If all this worry over drinking water sounds like a hassle, consider this: some of my most gratifying miniadventures have been the search for and discovery of freshwater sources. Some of the most interesting areas on a saltwater trip are the intertidal zones where fresh water meets the sea. In the Pacific Northwest, such waters contain prized sport fish like the sea-run cutthroat. And crabs are often found in bays that receive freshwater streams.

If salt water is your destination and your only recollections of the ocean are salt and sand in your bathing suit, a bad taste, and a terrible itch, I have some reassuring news. You can be clean and fresh in spite of it. You can wash your dishes in it, and most outdoors stores carry soaps that work well in salt water, though you might want to give them a quick rinse with fresh. There are saltwater soaps that you can bathe and shampoo with, and the best news of all: you can even buy a solar shower. Fill it with fresh or salt water in the morning, leave it in the sun, and in the evening you'll have a hot shower. But suppose you don't have a solar shower, and your freshwater supply is extremely limited. You can bathe and rinse in salt water; just make sure you towel off quickly. The itch comes only if you allow the salt water to evaporate on your skin, leaving its residue of salt.

No, you can't drink the stuff, and *don't* try to run it through the purifier. But an ounce or two in the fresh water to speed up the boil of your oatmeal or spaghetti is okay. Early in my sea kayaking apprenticeship, a couple of my experienced friends told me I could create fresh water from salt water by straining it through a colander lined with salt grass. I almost fell for it; these are the kind of friends that invite you on snipe hunts.

ON THE BEACH

For many of us, the real allure of sea kayaking is the beach. It may be in a small protected bay or on an exposed coast. Considering the cost of beachfront property, it's not surprising how much this means to most folks. The shores of New Jersey and Southern California notwithstanding, a beach can absorb a tremendous amount of human abuse; Mother Nature will renew and replenish it. On many outside beaches, the abundance of wood is both a blessing and a curse. Huge logs can serve as part of your shelter construction; but they can also clog up streams and obliterate otherwise hospitable beaches. I have camped on many beaches in the Pacific Northwest where the profusion of wood shapes and sizes, including dimensional lumber, allows for some incredibly creative beach architecture. Firewood can be scooped up in kindling or Yule-log sizes within a few yards of your fire.

Yes, fires. There may be certain areas where wood is scarce or where for other reasons open fires are restricted. In the wilder coastal areas, however, as soon as you get beyond the most heavily trafficked shores, the supply seems infinite. Still, this is not an invitation to build giant beach fires, especially those that leave black scars and charred logs behind. Beaches, like any backcountry camping site, deserve the low impact consideration contained in the admonition "Take only pictures, leave only footprints."

A major plague on the beaches is the litter of seemingly thousands of plastic bottles and other detritus. They are invariably the garbage of powerboaters, both recreational and commercial. Since they have a half-life of maybe 20,000,000 years, there is a case to be made for this fetish of one of my paddling friend's: he finds deserted beaches, spends an hour collecting all the plastic

Your own beachfront property at an affordable price

flotsam, then incinerates it on the beach. A huge pile is reduced to a small gooey blob in minutes. The toxic mushroom cloud that this act produces seems a small price to pay for cleaner beaches, and it is hardly recommended (and probably illegal) in all but the most remote areas. Needless to say, carry out your own cans, bottles, litter, and maybe a few of those plastic castaways.

Sand and gravel beaches are natural septic systems; it's easy to dig a drain hole for your "gray water," and this is probably okay in remote areas. For other kinds of waste, whatever can't be burned needs to be carried out. Human waste, in the absence of toilets or outhouses, must be buried in the woods well away from the beach. In remote areas, human waste may be deposited below the tide line. In certain ecologically sensitive areas, or in areas that bear fairly heavy traffic, the use of portable potties, ammo cans, and the like may be necessary.

Which brings us to an issue of tremendous sensitivity.

THE KAYAK INVASION

The kayak, which is so stealthy and inviting to us as paddlers, can create problems far larger than their small size would suggest. Beachfront property is indeed valuable, and those who own it are quite protective of it. The sight of a kayak—worse yet, a small flotilla—landing on someone's prized beach can create major public relations problems. When the crew are seen relieving themselves in strategic locations, landowners may lose their cool. In some states—Hawaii, for example—*all* beaches are public property. Where beaches are public, the high-tide mark may be

the delineator. This means that you may find beaches where you can stop and have a picnic but where camping above the tide mark (a wise plan!) may put you into Farmer Brown's field. Just as it is with any other law, it's your job to know what's public and what's private. As more and more kayakers take to the water, it must become second nature to us to familiarize ourselves with our routes, and to know what beaches, landings, or islands may be off limits. These little boats, which we consider to be environmentally, even socially, nonintrusive, are capable of stirring the wrath of enough people that we may find ourselves, at some future date, subject to licensing, taxes, and regulations, all of which can take the fun out of a kayaker's life.

Private landowners are not the only potential victims of our invasions. Many public areas are also off limits. Some of these are bird and wildlife sanctuaries. The restricted status of such areas should be clear enough. What may not be so clear is that in all of the areas where we are free to travel, the bird and mammal life, which is one of the chief attractions of kayaking, may be put at risk by our intrusions. Whether it is sea lions, seals, cranes, ducks, or bears, keep your distance. In some cases your "stealth" can be a traumatic event for your feathered or furry friend.

I am not prepared to evaluate the reverse situation—your own safety—but I recently heard the following unconfirmed story. A kayaker was noticed by persons on shore to be "harassing" a whale by continually pursuing it in his kayak and whacking the water with his paddle blade. Other than observing to themselves that kayakers must be jerks, they didn't give the incident another thought. A year later, this story was overheard by a local paddle sports retailer. What the listener knew, and what the shore dwellers did not, was that in the very vicinity of the reported harassment, a kayaker had disappeared and was never seen again. His undamaged kayak, on rental from a local shop, had been recovered nearby. Possible conclusion: an orca (a mammal fully capable of reasoned action but with no known, documented record of attacks on humans) carefully separated the kayaker from his boat and dispatched him. True or not, it is a good story with a powerful moral.

Where rivers meet the sea—and open ocean beyond

APPENDIX

OCEAN KAYAKING FLOAT PLAN

Name and phone number of Kayaker(s):

(Use back of sheet for additional persons.)

(1) _____ _____

(2) _____ _____

(3) _____ _____

(4) _____ _____

Descriptions of Kayaks:

(Deck color, hull color, length)

(1) _____

(2) _____

(3) _____

(4) _____

Colors of expected paddling clothes:

(1) _____

(2) _____

(3) _____

(4) _____

Trip Expectations:

Put in location: _____

Take out location: _____

Approximate route: _____

Latest expected return date: _____

If Overdue or In Case of Emergency,

Name & Telephone of Contact Person: _____ _____

Radio: AM/FM Receiver _____, Shortwave Receiver _____

Aircraft Frequency Transmitter _____ Marine Band Transmitter _____

ELT or EPIRB _____.

Survival Equipment: Tent Style & Color _____,

First Aid Kit _____, Spare Paddle _____, Flares _____, Smoke _____,

Panels _____, Weapons _____.

Auto Description/License #: _____

Where Parked _____

Any Other Information _____

BOOKS

Instruction and General

Burch, David. *Fundamentals of Kayak Navigation.* Chester, Conn.: Globe Pequot Press, 1987. 283 pp. Bibl. Index.

Dowd, John. *Sea Kayaking:* A Manual for Long-distance Touring, rev. ed. Vancouver, B.C.: Douglas & McIntyre; Seattle: University of Washington Press, 1988. 303 pp. Illus. Bibl. Index.

Hutchinson, Derek C. *Derek C. Hutchinson's Guide to Sea Kayaking.* Chester, Conn.: Globe Pequot Press, 1985. 122 pp. Illus. Index.

Hutchinson, Derek. *Eskimo Rolling.* Camden, Me.: International Marine Publishing, 1988. 152 pp. Illus. Index.

Seidman, David. *The Essential Sea Kayaker: A Complete Course for the Open Water Traveler.* Camden, Me.: International Marine Publishing, 1992. 144 pp. Illus.

Washburne, Randel. *The Coastal Kayaker's Manual:* A Complete *Guide to Skills, Gear, and Sea Sense.* Chester, Conn.: Globe Pequot Press, 1989. 226 pp. Illus. Bibl. Index.

Guidebooks

Carey, Neil G. *A Guide to the Queen Charlotte Islands.* Anchorage: Alaska Northwest Publishing, 1975–. Annual.

DuFresne, Jim. *Glacier Bay National Park.* Seattle: The Mountaineers, 1987. 152 pp. Illus. Maps.

Horwood, Dennis, and Tom Parkin. *Islands for Discovery: An Outdoor Guide to B.C.'s Queen Charlotte Islands.* Victoria, B.C.: Orca Book Publishers, 1989. 200 pp. Illus. Maps.

Ince, John, and Heidi Kottner. *Sea Kayaking Canada's West Coast.* Vancouver, B.C.: Raxas Books, 1982. 240 pp. Illus. Maps. Index.

Miller, David William. *A Guide to Alaska's Kenai Fjords,* 2nd ed. Cordova, AK: Wilderness Images, 1987. 116 pp. Illus. Bibl. Index.

Snowden, Mary Ann. *Island Paddling: A Paddler's Guide to the Gulf Islands and Barkley Sound.* Victoria, B.C.: Orca Publishers, 1990. 200 pp. Illus.

Sutherland, Chuck, ed. *Northeastern Coastal Paddling Guide.* Tuckahoe, N.Y.: Association of North Atlantic Kayakers, 1984. 39 pp. Illus. Maps.

Washburne, Randel. *The Coastal Kayaker: Kayak Camping on the Alaska and B.C. Coast.* Seattle: Pacific Search Press, 1983. 214 pp. Illus. Maps. Bibl. Index.

Washburne, Randel. *Kayaking Puget Sound, the San Juans, and Gulf Islands: 45 Trips on the Northwest's Inland Waters.* Seattle: Mountaineers, 1990. 224 pp. Illus. Bibl.

Washburne, Randel. *Kayak Trips in Puget Sound and the San Juan Islands.* Seattle: Pacific Search Press, 1986. 153 pp. Illus. Maps. Bibl.

Weaverling, Charles K. *Kayak Routes and Camping Beaches in Western and Central Prince William Sound, Alaska.* 1987. Available from Wild Rose Guidebooks.

Ziegler, Ronald. *Wilderness Waterways: A Whole Water Reference for Paddlers.* Kirkland, Wash.: Canoe America Associates, 1991. 177 pp. (Bibliography and source book for most of the entries in this Appendix)

MAGAZINES

Atlantic Coastal Kayaker

29 Burley St.
Wenham, MA 01984

Canoe Magazine

P.O. Box 3146
Kirkland, WA 98083
1-800-MY CANOE

Folding Kayaker

P.O. Box 0754
Planetarium Station
New York, NY 10024

Kayak Touring

P.O. Box 3146
Kirkland, WA 98083
1-800-MY CANOE

Paddler Magazine

4061 Oceanside Blvd., Suite M
Oceanside, CA 92056
303-879-1450

Sea Kayaker

6327 Seaview Ave. N.W.
Seattle, WA 98107-2664
206-789-7350

ORGANIZATIONS

Maine Island Trail Association
P.O. Box 8, 41A Union Wharf
Portland, ME 04101

ANORAK (Association of North Atlantic Kayakers)
34 East Queens Way
Hampton, VA 23669

TASK (Trade Association of Sea Kayaking)
P.O. Box 84144
Seattle, WA 98124

MAPS AND CHARTS

National Oceanic and Atmospheric Administration
National Ocean Service, Distribution Branch
Riverside, MD 20737-119
(301)436-6990
Publishes charts for waters surrounding the United States and its possessions. A free index is available. NOAA also publishes a series of *United States Coast Pilots*.

United States Geological Survey
National Mapping Division
National Center
12201 Sunrise Valley Dr.
Reston, VA 22092
(703) 648-6131
Free index. Topographic maps useful for coastal areas where land features (like trails, roads, etc.) are important to an itinerary.

Environment Canada, Canadian Hydrographic Service
Institute of Ocean Sciences
P.O. Box 8080
Ottawa, K1G 3H6, Canada
(613) 998-4931
Charts for all the Great Lakes and Canadian coastal waters.

Nongovernment Sources and Dealers

Bovey Marine Ltd., 375 water St., Vancouver, BC V6B 3J5 (604)685-8216 Chart Dealer.

Dominion Map Ltd., 541 Howe St., Vancouver, BCV 6C2 Mapmaker, map dealer.

Gabriel Aero Marine Instruments, 1490 Lower Water St., Halifax, NS B3J 2R7 (902)423-7252; 351 St. Paul St. W., Montreal, PQ H2Y 2A7 (514)845-8342 Chart dealer.

McGill Maritime Services, 369 Place d'Youville, Montreal, PQ H2Y 2G2 (514)849-1125 Chart dealer.

Maritime Services Ltd., 3440 Bridgewater St., Vancouver, BC V5K 1B6 (604)294-4444 Chart dealer.

Ocean River Sports, 1437 Store St., Victoria, BC V8W 3J6 (604)381-4233 Chart dealer.

American Nautical Services Navigation Center, 514 Biscayne Blvd., Miami, FL 33132 (305)358-1414 Chart dealer.

Bahai Mar Marine Store, 801 Seabreeze Blvd., Fort Lauderdale, FL 33316 (305)764-8831 Chart dealer.

Baker, Lyman and Co., 3220 1–10 Service Rd., W., Metairie, LA 70001 (504)831-3685; 8876 Gulf Fwy. Suite 110 Houston, TX 77007 (713)943-7032 Chart dealer.

Boxells Chandlery, 68 Long Wharf, Boston, MA 02110 (617)523-5678 Chart dealer.

W.T. Brownley Co., 118 W. Plume St., Norfolk, VA 23510 (804)622-7589 Chart dealer.

Captains Nautical Supplies, 138 N.W. 10th St., Portland, OR 97209 (503)227-1648; 1914 Fourth Ave., Seattle, WA 98101 (800)448-2278 Chart dealer.

McCurnin Nautical Charts Co., 2318 Woodlawn Ave., Metairie, LA 70001 (504)888-4500 Chart dealer.

Maryland Nautical Sales, 1143 Hull St., Baltimore, MD 21230 (301)752-4268 Chart dealer.

New York Nautical Instrument and Service Corp., 140 W. Broadway, New York, NY 10013 (212)962-4522 Chart dealer.

Pacific Map Center, 647 Auahi St., Honolulu, HI 96813 (808)531-3800 Chart dealer.

Safe Navigation Inc., 107 E. 8th St., Long Beach, CA 90813 (213)590-8744 Chart dealer.

Southwest Instruments Co., 235 W. 7th St., San Pedro, CA 90731 (213)519-7800 Chart dealer.

Tradewind Instruments Ltd., 2540 Blanding Ave., Alameda, CA 94501 (415)523-5726 Chart dealer.

CLUBS, ASSOCIATIONS, NEWSLETTERS

ALASKA

Knik Kanoers and Kayakers Inc., c/o Jeanne Molitor, P.O. Box 101935, Anchorage, AK 99510 (907)272-9351

BRITISH COLUMBIA

British Columbia Kayak and Canoe Club, 1606 W. Broadway, Vancouver, BC, Canada V6S 1S8.

CALIFORNIA

Bay Area Sea Kayakers, c/o Penny Wells, 229 Courtright Rd., San Rafael, CA 94901 (415)457-6094

FLORIDA

Florida Sea Kayaking Association, c/o George Ellis, 3095 67th Ave. S., St. Petersburg, FL 33172 (813)864-2651

GEORGIA

Coastal Georgia Paddling Club, c/o Katie Goodwin, 505 Herb River Dr., Savannah, GA 31406.

HAWAII

(Virtually every town and village in Hawaii has an outrigger canoe club; and most members paddle surf skis.)

NEW YORK

Metropolitan Association of Sea Kayakers, c/o Al Ysaguirre, 195 Prince St, New York, NY 10012

TEXAS

Texas Sea/Touring Kayak Club, P.O. Box 27281, Houston, TX 77227 (Sherry Gillan: [713]660-7000)

WASHINGTON

Washington Kayak Club, c/o Kathy Anderson, P.O. Box 24264, Seattle, WA 98124 (206)788-7919

INDEX